African Violets

Tony Clements

(The African Violet Centre)

David & Charles

For Diana, Maggie & Alan

Photography Andrew Lawson
Illustrations Joyce Tuhill
Ms typing & correcting Sheila Catlin
Technical information Joan Hill & Gwen Goodship

British Library Cataloguing in Publication Data

Clements, Tony
  African violets
  1. African violets
  I. Title
  635.9'3381   SB413 A4

  ISBN 0-7153-9024 Hdbk
  ISBN 0-7153-9187-9 Pbk

First published 1988
Second impression 1989
Third impression 1990
Fourth impression 1992

Phototypeset by Typesetters (Birmingham) Ltd,
Smethwick, West Midlands
and printed in Great Britain
by Redwood Press Ltd, Melksham, Wilts
for David & Charles
Brunel House   Newton Abbot   Devon

Contents

Introduction:
All Year Round Charm

The popularity of the African violet is boundless. Its admirers and collectors stretch from the equator to the Arctic Circle. In the tropics, its original home, it will grow happily on a shady verandah; in more temperate climates it makes an ideal indoor flowering houseplant. The African violet, or *Saintpaulia* to give it its proper botanical name, is one of the very few genuine flowering houseplants, for while many other plants may be taken into the home after being brought into bloom in a greenhouse, the African violet will bud and bloom indoors. What is more, given the correct care and attention, its entire life-cycle from seedling to mature plant may be achieved in the home. This native of Africa is a very tolerant plant which will make an easy-going and undemanding companion, and be a source of delight, pleasure and interest for many years. It thrives on neglect, asking only for a warm and light position, and a drink of water when it wilts with dryness. Even in the smallest home, space can be found for this compact plant, where it will reward you with the beauty of its flowers, especially welcome during the dreary days of winter.

The choice of variety in African violets is now very wide indeed, with a colour range to suit all tastes. Those who like the traditional shades will take pleasure in the rich dark blues with a bold yellow eye. The delicate pastel shades of the pinks capture the hearts of many flower-lovers, while the simplicity of the pure whites always attracts admiration. If you prefer bolder colours, then the magenta-reds, lilacs and purples will take your eye.

One group of violets which has become increasingly

popular in recent years is the bi-colours. These striking flowers have petals marked with two or more colours, and in full bloom are really eye-catching. Two of the top-selling varieties in the African violet list are bi-colours. First in popularity comes 'Fancy Pants', whose white petals have a frilled magenta border; close on its heels comes 'Miss Pretty', its large white blossoms edged with pink. Also high in the popularity ratings are the blue-edged whites, such as 'China Cup'.

There are not only flowers consisting of white petals with coloured borders; there are also coloured blooms with a white border. These are known by collectors as 'Genevas', for reasons which will be explained later. Adding further variety to the bi-colours are those with white petals and a coloured centre, such as 'Jubilee' (blue centre) and 'Sunset' (magenta centre).

Some plants have flowers which are splashed with two colours, usually pink and blue. They are very unusual, and are known as 'fantasy' types. When propagated, it very frequently happens that the next generation will show up all blue or all pink. This is not only disappointing, but means that these plants do not lend themselves to commercial production, hence their rarity.

This tremendous range of colour types in African violets is matched by a wide range of forms. There are tiny micro-miniatures which will make themselves at home in a wine-glass. One of the most well known of these has a pale pink flower, and is named appropriately enough 'Pip Squeek'. Then there are plants whose leaves are streaked with white or yellow markings. Known as 'variegated' varieties, they are available with flowers in a wide range of colours. In the eyes of the uninitiated, these variegated plants are frequently thought to be diseased. At the African Violet Centre this imagined 'problem' has often been brought to my attention by well-meaning visitors. One of the advantages of the variegated varieties is that even when the plant is not in bloom, the colourful foliage continues to delight the eye.

Finally, there are the trailing violets. These are African

violets which have a branching and weeping or pendulous habit. They are most at home in a hanging basket, suspended on the inside of a window on the shady side of the house. In the course of a year or two, the stems and leaves of the plant will hang down to obscure the container and its blooms will provide a cascade of colour.

Trailers and miniatures, variegateds and bi-colours, African violets come in an endless range of colour and form. If the secrets of their care are learned, they will charm us the whole year round with the beauty of their flowers.

1
Out of The Dark Continent

To understand how this plant has adapted so readily to living and thriving in our homes, we need to examine its origins. In the wild, it occurs only in East Africa, growing in the Usambara mountains district of Tanzania. There, in its various forms, it may be found from the foothills right up to an altitude of more than 7,000ft (2,200m). Baron von St Paul (see overleaf) did not realise that the plant material he had sent to Germany represented not one but two species of this newly discovered plant. Even Wendland at the Royal Botanic Garden thought that all the plants were of *Saintpaulia ionantha*. It was only later that differences were noted between two groups of the plants, and it was then realised that here was not one species but two. The second was given the name *Saintpaulia confusa*.

This turned out to be a stroke of good fortune for it meant that by cross-breeding between *S. ionantha* and *S. confusa* the first hybrid seed could be produced. This would lead, in the years ahead, to an explosion of colour and form in the genus *Saintpaulia*.

The discoverer of this shy and retiring plant was an obscure colonial official working in an outpost of the German empire at the end of the nineteenth century. His name was Baron Walter von St Paul, and he was a colonial administrator in the East African territory of Tanganyika, known today as Tanzania. He was also an amateur botanist, but in his wildest dreams he could scarcely have imagined the prodigious popularity in store for this little plant. It was in 1892 that he sent to his father in Germany specimens of this plant he had discovered. In so doing he set it on the path which was to lead to it becoming the most popular flowering houseplant in the world.

Baron von St Paul snr successfully grew the plants in Germany, and their discovery was brought to the attention of Hermann Wendland, director of the Royal Botanic Garden at Herrenhausen, near Hanover. Wendland described this new and previously unrecorded plant in the magazine *Gartenflora* of 10 June 1893, and he it was who gave to it its proper botanical name. In honour of its discoverer it was given the genus name *Saintpaulia*, and because its flowers had a resemblance to those of the true violet, Wendland gave it the specie name *ionantha* (violet-flowered), so it came about that this delightful little plant was burdened with the Latin name '*Saintpaulia ionantha*'. Even Wendland thought this name too cumbersome for regular use and described the plant as the *Usambara veilchen* (violet). This is still the name in popular use to this day in Germany, *Usambara* recalling its original mountain home in Tanzania. In English-speaking countries it is known as the African violet, although it is no relation of the true violet. It belongs to the family Gesneriaceae, and among its cousins are achimenes, gloxinia and streptocarpus.

The natural home of the African violet is in the tropics, close to the equator. However, because it grows also at altitude, it is tolerant of temperatures lower than those prevailing in the tropical rain forest. In its natural habitat it is shaded from the fierceness of the sun by a canopy of trees. Where the canopy of protective trees is removed by felling and the land brought under cultivation, this natural habitat is

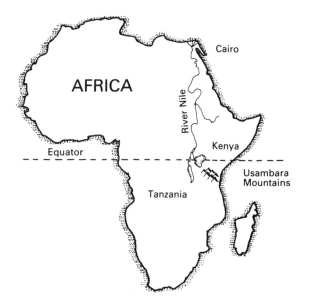

The home of the wild African violet lies in the Usambara mountains of Tanzania, close to the equator and south-west of Lake Victoria

---

destroyed and the *Saintpaulia* cannot survive. Unfortunately, this has caused the extinction in the wild of at least one of the species, *S. magungensis*, which today survives only in collections.

Farming considerations apart, this plant thrives where the temperature is a warm 68–77°F (20–25°C), with little night-time fluctuation, and where it is shaded from the fierceness of the sun. These conditions are also those found in our modern, centrally-heated homes. Little wonder, therefore, that the *Saintpaulia* has found in them a real home-from-home.

For the first thirty years or so after its discovery, the *Saintpaulia* was little more than a curiosity. Naturally, very little was known about its cultivation, its likes and dislikes, and initially poor results were experienced by those who tried to grow it. By the 1920s, however, interest in this plant

The true violet (top) belongs to the family Violaceae and makes its home in temperate climates (eg, The British Isles and North America). The *Saintpaulia* or African violet belongs to the family Gesneriaceae and is a native of the tropics

was increasing, and the first surge in its popularity can be pinpointed to the year 1927, for that was the year in which the Los Angeles, California, nursery of Armacost and Royston set the African violet on the road to popularity and success.

This was achieved by introducing and naming ten new hybrids. From Suttons of England and Benary of Germany they imported seed. This seed yielded more than one thousand seedlings, and from this number just ten plants were selected as having commercial value. All were in the blue/violet/purple colour range, and they were named as follows: Admiral, Amethyst, Blue Boy, Commodore, Mermaid, Neptune, Norseman, Number 32, Sailor Boy and Viking. Thus it came about that the first *named Saintpaulia* hybrids were offered for sale. All were grown from Suttons seed except for Blue Boy and Sailor Boy which came from Benary seed.

The beauty of these single blue/purple African violets proved irresistible. Thanks to a greater understanding of their cultural needs and also to the wider introduction of home central heating, they met with increasing success as houseplants and their popularity began to climb. Greater numbers were produced to meet the growing demand, and in order to stimulate public interest growers began to categorise violets according to their leaf types – round, pointed, serrated, and so on – for at this time the flowers, while not uniform in colour, offered nothing outside the blue/purple range.

Singles and Doubles

Until 1939 the only flowers ever seen on an African violet were blue and single. This was all set to change, however, in a very short space of time. The first significant mutation was discovered by a Michigan grower Ed Wangbichler. In a batch of plants of Blue Boy he was growing in 1939, he came across a sport never before seen: one plant was bearing beautiful *double* blue flowers. Each flower consisted of two

13

sets of petals, one on top of the other, giving a total number of ten petals instead of the normal five. Not only did this make an unusual and attractive plant, it also had considerable significance for the commercial future of the African violet, for it was soon realised that this double-flowered sport did not drop its blooms and therefore would make a long-lasting display of flowers. All the singles had the drawback of dropping their blossoms as soon as they were fully open. This was a real problem for the commercial grower because by the time his African violet plants had been transported to the flower shop, many of the flowers had fallen off.

It would take a further twenty-five years for this problem to be solved. Not until the 1960s was a strain of apparently single violets introduced which retained their petals and were genuinely 'non dropping'. To assign the credit for this we have to return to Baron von St Paul's native Germany, to the Isselburg nursery of Hermann Holtkamp and his highly successful commercial strain of 'Rhapsodie' *Saintpaulia*.

The Colour Breakthrough

Blue Boy, which had surprised violet growers with its double-flowered mutation, had another trick up its sleeve. In the following year, 1940, it was to produce a totally unexpected and astonishing mutation. In that year another batch of Blue Boy yielded a unique treasure of a sport in the greenhouses of Holton and Hunkel in Milwaukee, USA. There on the bench amid a sea of blue, there shone out a single clear *pink* flower. You may imagine the surprise and delight on the face of the first grower to spot it. This was the first true pink violet ever seen. It was given the name 'Pink Beauty' and marked a distinct colour breakthrough.

'Boy' and 'Girl' Violets

In 1939 there had occurred a Blue Boy sport with double flowers. The following year another Blue Boy sport had produced pink flowers. In 1941 Blue Boy produced its third

14

surprise. This time it was not the flower that was different, but the leaf. The leaves on this plant were quite different from the plain, standard green of the normal Blue Boy. These leaves were rounded, thicker, slightly wavy, with a striking yellow/white patch on the leaf-base where it joined the stalk. This sport was given the name 'Blue Girl', and ever since then this type of leaf has been known as 'girl-type'. At the time of writing, a commercial series, widely grown in Europe and known as the 'Rococo' series, is notable for having compact girl-type foliage.

The term 'boy' or 'girl' has nothing whatever to do with the sex of the plants. African violets are bi-sexual, the flowers containing both stamen and pistil, that is, male and female organs. Individual flowers without stamens are sometimes seen, epecially in doubles. The term refers, in fact, simply to the type of leaf.

Mutations and Sports

Up to this point in the story of the African violet, the new developments of double blooms, pink flowers and girl-type leaf have all occurred as mutations or sports. When a new plant differs noticeably from its parents, it is called a 'sport' or 'mutation'. It is the result of a sudden variation in characteristics, a change in the properties of a single gene, and appears in an accidental or random way. It is not the result of human interference.

However, plant breeders or hybridisers now began to realise that in the *Saintpaulia* they had stumbled across a genetic treasure house. If new forms and different colours could occur by accident, surely with a little help even greater wonders might be achieved. The hybridisers were about to unlock this treasure house and they were to have a field day. The first to put his name in the record books was Peter Ruggeri who had been patiently and diligently hybridising in San Francisco. His endeavours were rewarded in 1942 when he produced the first pure white seedling, which he named 'White Lady'.

15

Fifty years after the discovery of the original *S. ionantha* growing on the slopes of the Usambara mountains, the plant stood on the threshold of worldwide popularity and success. Available now in blue (single and double), pink and white, it was all set to colonise our homes. The number of enthusiastic collectors was growing steadily in the United States, where the first show dedicated solely to African violets was held in November 1946. This was in Atlanta, Georgia, and attracted the remarkable attendance of nine thousand visitors in two days. Out of this gathering was formed the nucleus of the African Violet Society of America, whose first annual convention was held in 1947, also in Atlanta.

The AVSA can claim the distinction of having fostered the growing interest in African violet collecting and of having encouraged the determined endeavours of hybridisers to strive to produce new colour variations and larger flowers. Results came in thick and fast. An entirely new trend appeared in 1950, the first plant with petals edged in white. Its flower was purple, edged with white; it was raised at the Geneva nurseries in California and was given the name 'Lady Geneva'. Henceforth all hybrids, double or single, having white-edged petals, have been known as 'Genevas'.

Among some Geneva crosses, at about this time, there appeared the first true *miniature* African violet. It was given the name 'Miss Liberty'.

Seeing Stars

In 1952 a new flower shape came on the scene. This was the first star-flowered violet, whose petals were all of equal size, and which thus resembled a five-pointed star. The first one was, not surprisingly, purple in colour and named 'Purple Star'. The significance of this development is that star flowers are generally larger than the standard flowers, and thus enable the plant to make a more strikingly colourful impact.

While all this activity had been going on in America, in Tanganyika things had also been moving on apace. Baron von St Paul's 1892 discoveries, *S, ionantha* and *S. confusa*, had

16

The 'regular' African violet flower (left) has two smaller upper petals, and two pairs of pollen sacs. The 'star' flower has five pointed petals, of equal size, and five pairs of pollen sacs

been joined by a further eighteen species, collected from the same region. One of these was *S. grotei*, a 1920 discovery, which displays a climbing or weeping habit and is able to grow to a length of 3ft (1m). In the early 1950s Frank and Anne Tinari of Philadelphia used *S. grotei* in their hybridising programme, resulting in the first 'trailer' hybrids. These have a branching and pendulous habit and make an ideal subject for a hanging basket.

The first double pink African violet was introduced in 1954 by Lyndon Lyon of Dolgeville, New York, and at this point the basic range of violets we have today was fairly well established.

The appeal of these charming houseplants has been widened since by the advent of frilled flowers, non-dropping singles and a wide range of enchanting bi-colours. However, at the time of writing we still await flowers in the yellow, orange and scarlet sector of the colour spectrum. One attribute of the unrelated true violet missing in the *Saintpaulia* is a fragrance, and it seems unlikely that it ever will have any scent. But in the botanical laboratories of the future it may be that genetic engineering will equip the African violets of the twenty-first century with a perfume. What a delight that would be! We can only await further developments with interest and anticipation.

17

2
Plant Care:
'African Violets Die on Me!'

To grow and flower African violets successfully requires a certain amount of care and knowledge. Most people have no difficulty in growing a plant with plenty of green leaves, but persuading a healthy-looking plant to send out some flowers is not so easy. This obviously is the object of keeping violets, and it is somewhat frustrating to have a house full of plants without blooms. Luck does not really play any part in it, but being 'green-fingered' does. This know-how is something which can be cultivated; you can learn to be green-fingered because this accomplishment is simply an awareness of the needs of your plants.

Just as pet owners build up a rapport with their dog or cat, getting to know their likes and dislikes, so a similar awareness can be built up with regard to plants. It is then possible to determine if they are happy or unhappy, in good health or deteriorating, and to take remedial steps if necessary. After all, houseplants do become 'honorary' pets. Plant owners become concerned for their health and happiness, cannot bear to part with them even when they are old

18

and no longer beautiful, and are upset and reproach themselves when they die. It is hardly possible to take them to the
vet, so you must learn enough about their needs to doctor
them yourself.

Each and every plant is an individual, with its own
particular needs at its own particular time. Even though you
may have several plants of the same variety, they will require
individual treatment. One specimen may be large and
growing away vigorously, and this will need regular
watering and strong feeding; another plant may be less
strong with a smaller root system, and this will need only
occasional watering and dilute feeding. It is such a temptation
to feed and water all your violets at one and the same time,
whether they are all ready for it or not. The inevitable result
is that the slower-growing plants cannot take it, are
overcome by waterlogging, and drown.

'I can't get on with African violets, they die on me!' That
*anguished cry is frequently heard from visitors to the African
Violet Centre. Maybe it is the colourful sight of thousands of
healthy violets in bloom which induces in some folk feelings of
inadequacy and despair. The truth is not that violets generally die
on people, but that many people kill them. The favourite method
of destruction is drowning. The evidence indicates that over-
watering is the major cause of premature death in all houseplants.
African violets are especially vulnerable because their water
requirement is small.*

In this chapter you will find suggestions and tips about the
care of violets, based on the writer's own experience and that
of many other violet lovers. There are a thousand and one
ways of caring for plants, and if your system is successful, then
please do not change it just because it appears to conflict with
the advice in these pages. African violets all have similar
needs, but the homes in which they grow vary enormously
in temperature, light and humidity, and in the life-styles of
their owners. It is therefore not possible to give precise
instructions like, for example, 'water every two weeks',
because conditions vary not only from house to house, but

also from room to room within the same house. If the room temperature is a steady 73°F (23°C) and dry, then the violet may need a weekly watering; but if the room is only at 60°F (15°C), then the plant will probably last for three or four weeks before it dries out and needs a drink. So the instructions given here will relate to the principles of basic care which you must interpret according to your own particular circumstances.

Given the correct attention, African violets can be remarkably long-lived. There are many reports of plants living to fifteen or twenty years and even one which was claimed to be thrity-two years old. Usually these plants were received as a gift to mark a special occasion, such as the birth of a daughter, and thus their age can be accurately dated. As long as violets are well cared for, they will certainly give pleasure for several years. In providing a home for an African violet, we hope to have a plant which not only looks a picture of health, but will regularly provide a colourful display of its beautiful flowers. The advice in the following pages is planned to help in the achievement of this goal.

It has been rather cynically suggested in some quarters that the last thing the professional grower wants is for his African violets to last a long time once they've been sold. These same snide voices claim that it is in the grower's interests that the customers kill off their violets as soon as possible, thus having to return to buy more and boosting the grower's sales. Such suggestions are not only mischievous, but betray a lack of understanding of human nature, for if too many people experience too little success with their plants, they will refuse to buy more and give the African violet a bad name.

On the other hand, if those who take violets home with them find that they are rewarding plants to grow and give a great deal of satisfaction, they will be well pleased. Indeed, these satisfied customers will be so delighted that they will tell their friends about them and there will be an increase in the popularity of African violets. These same friends will be persuaded that they, too, must have such a plant in their home, and in this way the grower's sales will increase. A satisfied customer makes for a satisfied and successful grower – so much for the cynics!

In order to give of its best and to reward you for your care, the African violet has just four basic needs which must be supplied. They are: water, light, warmth and food. Everything else is peripheral and of minor importance. Some writers on African violets give the impression that to grow them successfully is a very complex and difficult procedure. They list complicated formulas for special compost, recommend particular nutrient formulations and give guidelines which are really more appropriate to the intensive-care unit of a hospital. For those folk who want to make African violet growing a way of life, these detailed instructions and formulations may well be of consuming interest; but to the general householder who simply wants to have a few colourful, healthy plants around the place, they are irrelevant. Be assured that excellent results may be obtained by noting the simple and basic recommendations which follow here.

TOP- OR BOTTOM-WATERING
Now we come to the vexed question of how to administer the water. There are those who claim that violets should always be watered from the top to avoid the accumulation of salts; others swear by bottom-watering, alleging that top-watering flushes out the plant's food nutrients. Each side can make out a convincing case to confirm the rightness of its method.

The truth is that either method will produce excellent results. What really matters is that the water is supplied only when the plant needs it, and that the compost in the pot is given a thorough soaking. The watering of your violets, whether from the top or the bottom, must be carried out carefully and thoroughly.

If top-watering is practised, great care must be taken to avoid getting water on the leaves or in the crown. Cold water splashed on to the leaves may kill the green chlorophyll,

(continued on page 24)

21

Correct Watering – The Key to Success

There can be no doubt that the key to successful violet growing lies in the correct watering of the plants. The water which maintains life can also become the water which brings death by drowning. The balance between the two is a fine one, but once you have mastered the watering of your plants, all the rest is relatively plain sailing. There is a rule for watering African violets, which is simple to practise and will ensure that the plants in your care never drown. The rule is this: never water an African violet until it *begs* for a drink. Wait until it wilts. These plants thrive on neglect, so wait until the leaves lose their crispness and begin to wilt. They may be dumb, but they can still tell you when they would like a drink; they signal with their leaves, allowing them to become limp.

Now at this point it is important to check that the compost is dry. Note that this should be carried out *after* you have received a signal from the plant that it is thirsty, and not before. Most writers suggest that you test the top of the compost daily to see if it is dry and water accordingly. This imposes on us a very subjective decision, full of uncertainty. Even when you are sure the compost in the top of the pot is dry, very often the rest of the compost and the root-ball is still moist. After all, it is the plant which needs the water; the compost is simply a means of making it available to the roots. So do not test the compost until the plant sends you the distress signal.

At this point you need to confirm that the wilting means 'I'm thirsty', and that it does not mean 'I'm drowning' or 'I'm under a disease attack' or 'I've got a chill' – the vocabulary of the African violet is rather limited. First, test the soil in the pot to see if it feels dry. Lift the pot and test its weight. If it is a plastic pot and the soil is dry, it will be very light indeed; if the compost is really dry it may even be shrinking away from the side of the pot. Should you find that the compost is wet and the pot heavy, then you may quite rightly assume that your plant's distress is caused by waterlogging. The very last thing it wants in this condition is more water, which will lead to certain death. It needs, in fact, the opposite and should be dried out in the warmest position available. Waterlogging excludes the air from the compost and the roots, which leads to irreversible and progressive root death. Recovery depends upon rapid drying out.

Most people assume that when a violet wilts, it needs water. This is only the case when the wilt is caused by dryness. In cold climates, when an African violet is purchased and carried home from a warm nursery or flower shop, it may be chilled on the way. On a winter's day of freezing temperatures, I have frequently seen customers carry plants out of a greenhouse at 68°F (20°C) and place them straight into the boot of their car, where the temperature is close to freezing point. Such plants, if left in this situation for more than a few minutes, are doomed. Their wilt will be an irreversible collapse. A cold shock may not, however, always be fatal, but it will always produce a wilt which usually does not happen until one or two days after the chilling experience. Examination of the compost will soon indicate that the cause is not drought, and that its recovery requires a warm room, not more water.

Having established that your violet plant's wilt is caused not by waterlogging, disease or a chill, but by thirst, then you may give it a generous drink of water. Once it is really dry, then it needs a good long drink of warm (room temperature) water. Remember that the natural home of your violet is the tropics, where the rain-water is warm. They certainly dislike the shock of having their roots immersed in cold tap-water. Such a shock will slow down their growth and even cause brown spots on the leaf. There is nothing wrong with using tap-water, but mix in a little from the hot tap so that the water you use is just warm to the touch.

leaving unsightly white spots and streaks. Should the crown of the plant become wet, it must be dried out quickly or it may start to rot. Warm water splashed on a leaf will cause no damage by itself, but if the rays of the sun should fall on it, the water acts like a magnifying lens causing brown burn marks on the leaf. So if you accidentally spill water on to your plant, make sure to take it out of sunlight until it has dried off.

The safest way to water from the top is to use a small watering-can with a long slender spout, which may be poked under the leaves, allowing the water to be poured directly on to the compost. One serious drawback to top-watering, however, is that it is very difficult to re-wet compost which has thoroughly dried out, for, as the compost dries, it contracts and shrinks away from the side of the pot. So water applied from above will simply run down the inside, and out through the drainage holes at the bottom without penetrating the soil. If top-watering is practised, care should be taken in these circumstances to see that the compost really does become re-moistened.

> *Bottom-watering is certainly simpler and enables a really dry plant to be revived rapidly. The easiest way to do this is to fill the kitchen sink to a depth of 2in (5cm) with tepid/warm water. Stand your thirsty violet in the water, which should come about half-way up the pot. Allow it to stand for thirty minutes, then remove from the water, drain and return to its saucer or pot-cover. This treatment should ensure that all the compost in the pot has received a good wetting to the benefit of the entire root system.*

While the kitchen-sink treatment is fine if you have only a few plants, it can become very time-consuming if you have a large collection. For this reason many African violet collectors water their plants via the saucers in which they stand, topping up the water until the plant takes up no more. After half an hour the remaining water should be emptied out. African violets are not pond plants; they are not aquatic, and do not enjoy having cold, wet feet. In this way many plants become waterlogged and drown. A further problem associated with watering via the saucer is that it can prove unsatisfactory if the compost in the pot does not readily absorb water. In that case, you will find that only the bottom inch of compost has become moistened, leaving the top two-thirds dry. The roots in this dry area will die, leaving a very restricted root system to support the plant. The results of this are seen frequently in sluggish plant growth and short flower stalks which can hardly raise the blooms above the leaves – the plant, in fact, is only firing on one cylinder!

There can be no doubt that to be sure of thoroughly moistening the compost, the kitchen-sink system, or an adaptation of it, produces the most effective results.

> *Tap-water is fine to use* except *if it has been through a water-softener, for although this removes the hard salts like calcium from the water, in the process sodium is released into the water. While this is harmless for humans to drink and has no taste, it will accumulate in the soil of pot plants, and, if used for a prolonged period, will reach a level of toxicity at which the plant will be poisoned. So use non-softened tap-water or rain-water. If you live in a hot and humid region you may have air-conditioners and dehumidifiers to make life more comfortable. The moisture which the systems remove from the air is pure water and may be used for your plants.*

Young plants, freshly potted, need rather careful treatment. Since they have as yet only a small root system, care must be taken to see that they are not overwhelmed by more water than they can cope with. It is better, therefore, to water sparingly from the top, applying the water to the soil where the roots are growing without saturating the whole pot. The roots of a young plant may not be able to handle such a quantity of moisture and may be drowned.

There is another reason why young plants should be watered sparingly. The aim with such a young plant is to build up a large, strong and healthy root system, capable of maintaining the plant in its maturity and supporting a large leaf area with a good head of blooms. If the young plant is deprived of water, the effect will be to cause its roots to go in

(continued on page 28)

Holiday Watering

For those violet growers who have established a satis-factory watering programme, holidays can produce a hiccough in the system. The most commonly heard horror-story about vacation time stars the well-intentioned neighbour in the role of the villain. I am sure the scenario is familiar to you. A friend or neighbour agrees to look after your house in your absence, checking round every day or two to make sure all is well. Their eye alights upon your African violets. In the absence of any specific instructions, they wonder whether the plants ought to be given some water. Invariably, these good neighbours feel that if in doubt, give a little drink. So your African violets which were accustomed to receiving water once every two weeks, are suddenly being watered daily. Not sur-prisingly, they cannot take it, and two weeks is time enough to drown a violet. You return from your holiday sun-tanned and relaxed, to find your prized collection flagging round their pots under sentence of death.

There is, however, a solution to the problem. On the day before you go away, give your violets a prolonged soak in a bowl of water (the kitchen-sink treatment) so that they are well and truly saturated, then stand them in the centre of a room on the shady side of the house. In that way they should not become too hot, nor will they be subject to the sunlight on their leaves. Finally, write a clear notice, in capital letters, for the person looking after your home while you are away: 'Please do not water my violets'. That should do the trick. Now you may go off for your two weeks' holiday, or even extend it to four, knowing that when you return your violets may be dry, but will be perfectly safe. On your return, repeat the soaking treatment, and within a day the leaves will perk up and your plants will be fine.

A winter holiday can present a greater threat to the health of your African violets than one in the summer, especially if it coincides with a period of freezing weather conditions. If in your absence your home is without heat during severely cold weather, then the plants may die as a result of the low temperatures. The most satisfactory solution may be to take them to the home of a friend for safe keeping while you are away. However, if they have to remain at home, what can be done to keep them safe and hopefully preserve them until your return?

First, they should be placed in the centre of a sunny room, well away from the window. Even winter sun can have a warming effect, and that extra heat plus the brighter light, will benefit your violets.

Secondly, if the compost is on the dry side the plants will be better able to withstand low temperatures. Experience shows that plants which are very moist are the first to fall victim to the cold. It may, therefore, be wiser to withhold water from your violets before going away and leave them unwatered until your return. When you come home from your vacation they may well look wilted and bedraggled, but a good soak in tepid water should soon revive them.

search of moisture. This is the way in which its root system will be built up. If, on the other hand, the plant is over-watered, it will not need to send out its roots in search. Its root system will remain restricted and immature, unable to support a strong and vigorous plant. The result will be a poor-looking African violet, small in size with limp leaves which have a grey appearance. Any flowers it produces will be smaller than normal, growing on very short stems.

Humidity

Some years ago word was put about that the one thing above all else required for success with African violets was humidity. This idea was promoted so successfully in Britain that to this day the man in the street knows two things about African violets: they come from Africa and they need humidity. The average person is not quite clear about the exact meaning of 'humidity', but he knows it has to do with water. So if violets need humidity it must mean that they like lots of water. People in their thousands rushed off home to plunge their violets into bowls of shingle, sand, pebbles or peat, with the plastic pot base permanently in water. This gem of misinformation proved fatal to hundreds of thousands of otherwise healthy plants, resulting in mass drownings.

Humidity refers to the vapour content of the air around us. In the Tanzania home of the *Saintpaulia* not only is the temperature very warm, but the moisture content of the air is also high. Humidity may be measured by a hygrometer, and in its natural habitat the plant is accustomed to 70–80 per cent humidity. Commercially, they are grown at about 60 per cent humidity. The average centrally-heated home registers some 30 per cent humidity, and since thousands of people grow and bloom violets successfully in such conditions without any need to moisten that dry atmosphere, humidity levels cannot be of primary importance.

In most parts of the world, the air is by nature sufficiently moist for the needs of the African violet. Only in arid areas of very low rainfall and in deserts is it necessary to supplement the humidity level. During summertime the air is warmer and is able to hold more moisture than the cold air of winter. Since it is not necessary to heat our homes artificially in summer, it follows that the air in them is going to be more humid than in winter, when it is dried by our heating system. For this reason the provision of additional humidity will be of greater benefit in winter rather than summer.

It must be pointed out that many people who have African violets in the home find no need to give extra humidity. These plants are far more robust than we realise and grow in a perfectly satisfactory way standing in a dry saucer or pot-cover. This demonstrates clearly that high humidity is not vital to the life of the violet. There can be no doubt, nevertheless, that the nearer our growing conditions approximate to those in their native habitat, the happier they will be. It would not be possible to maintain in our homes a humidity level in excess of 70 per cent. We should find it far too oppressive for our own comfort; the walls would be running with condensation, the wallpaper would peel off and the carpets would go mouldy. It is quite unnecessary to attempt to raise the humidity level throughout the entire house; it is sufficient to raise the air moisture level in the immediate area of the plants. This is known as the creation of a micro-climate.

Before looking at ways of providing greater humidity for African violets, the effects of very low humidity on these plants should be considered. These effects are not life-threatening, but involve a lowering of the plant's performance. The leaves will lack their lustrous sheen, that glow of perfect health; even more important, very low humidity levels can inhibit the plant's ability to flower. The blooms it does produce will be sparse and small in size. If you seek perfection with your violets, then you will obviously wish to provide them with the best possible conditions, and if your home has a very dry atmosphere you will want to correct that for your plants.

In most homes there are two rooms at least where the air

moisture level is higher than in the rest of the house. These rooms are the kitchen and the bathroom, but their increased humidity will only benefit the violets if the plant's other and more vital needs are also being met. Many African violets bought to decorate the living-room have ended up blooming continuously on the kitchen windowsill. The steam given off by a boiling kettle and the various cooking activities keeps the humidity level up, providing just the sort of atmosphere in which violets thrive. Similarly, in the bathroom, the more frequently the members of the household run a bath or take a shower, the better your violets will like it.

What can be done to improve the conditions for the plants you wish to grow in rooms other than the kitchen or bathroom? First, by simply grouping your plants together, instead of standing them out singly, the humidity around them will be increased. The air between the leaves of the plants will hold more moisture and the plants themselves will not dry out so fast. In addition, you may provide extra humidity by standing the plants over a tray of moist shingle, pebbles or sand. Use a shallow, watertight tray or dish filled with shingle, pebbles or sand, which is kept moist with water at all times. The violets should be raised above this moist medium on a saucer or inverted plant pot. As the moisture evaporates from the tray, so the humidity of the air around the plants will be significantly increased.

One very important point is that on no account should the provision of extra humidity be confused with the activity of watering the plant. They are two totally separate operations. Additional humidity is provided by siting the plant above the moist sand or shingle, making certain that the base of the pot is not in contact with the moist medium, for if the bottom of the pot is actually touching the wet sand, then capillary action will ensure that the compost is constantly saturated with water. This will lead to the drowning of the roots and the collapse of the plant.

There are two further ways in which the humidity around your plants may be increased. Small dishes of water, placed beside the violets, will increase the humidity as the water in them evaporates. The other method favoured by some enthusiasts is to mist the plants. To be effective, this needs to be carried out daily, preferably early in the morning. Use a hand mister which produces very fine droplets of water, and use only sufficient to put a thin film of droplets on the violet. If you apply too much water so that it runs down the leaf stalk, it may gather on the crown and cause it to rot. For misting purposes use only warm water, and take care that the plants misted are not exposed to sunlight until they have dried off.

In conclusion, it is important to repeat that most people obtain quite satisfactory results from their African violets without taking any steps to increase the humidity. If you decide that you wish to enhance the beauty of your violets by increasing the moisture they receive through their leaf surfaces, do exercise caution.

Light – A Vital Ingredient

Most plant-lovers realise that if their houseplants are going to thrive, they need in various degrees water, food and warmth. What does not appear to be so widely understood is the vital need of all plants for light. Plants need light in order to live; without it they will die. Without the light of the sun, the Earth would be a barren planet. It is light which triggers the process of photosynthesis, by which plants manufacture the food they need for growth. Plants need light to live and grow much as we need air to breathe. If humans were deprived of oxygen in the air they breathed, they would die; if plants are deprived of light, they too will die.

African violets are particularly sensitive to the quality of light available and will only give of their best if the light intensity is to their liking. With poor and inadequate light, the African violet will be weedy and spindly and unable to flower. All the characteristics of the plant are affected by light: size of plant, length of leaf stalk, size of leaf and flower, number of blooms and even their colour. The artificial light in our homes enables us to see clearly, but it is totally

31

inadequate to assist in plant growth. Certainly there are plants, including African violets, which may be grown in artificial light. The source of such light needs to be a fluorescent tube and the violet must be exposed to it for 14–16 hours per day, at a distance of not more than 8in (20cm).

The question most frequently put to me about violet-growing is this: **'Why won't my African violet flower again? It is a healthy plant with plenty of lovely green leaves, but no flowers. Why?'** *Invariably, the answer is that the plant is receiving too little light. The light intensity is too weak for the plant to be able to initiate flower buds. Since too much light will scorch the plant and too little will lead to spindly growth and lack of flowers, you can tell when the light intensity is correct by means of a simple test. Place your hand between the plant and the sunlight; if a clear shadow is cast, then the light is too bright. This test applies only in the summer months; winter sunshine in temperate climates is fine for violets.*

You may take the view that since the *Saintpaulia* originates in the tropics, it should benefit from strong sunlight. Although there may seem to be logic in this opinion, in fact they choose to grow in positions shaded from the sun by trees or rocks. Indirect, filtered light from a summer sun is their natural preference. In commercial greenhouses the glass is heavily shaded during summer, reducing the light intensity by some 80 per cent. With the approach of winter, this shading is reduced until in Britain the plants are exposed to full sun from November to February. As the sun's power increases with the arrival of spring, repeated layers of shading are applied so that by midsummer the sun's power is again reduced by 80 per cent.

How can this commercial practice be adapted to the home situation? It would be somewhat unsightly to paint the windows white or green in summer, and it could well puzzle

---

A rare variegated sport of 'Fancy Pants'

An attractive un-named bi-coloured sport

your neighbours. Given that light is the key to keeping violets in bloom, it is important to ensure that they receive enough, but not too much. A great deal depends upon the latitude in which you live, and you will have to be guided by trial and error. In Great Britain, at approximately 52°N, the basic pattern is as follows: the plants stand in a sunny window during the winter half of the year and spend the summer in a window on the shady side of the house.

It is particularly important that the African violet should be placed close to the glass so that it is almost touching the window. The amount of light falling on the plant is reduced considerably if it stands very far from the glass. If you stand a violet on a table in the centre of the room to enjoy it to the full, it will be reasonably happy there for a few weeks, although its flowers will become rather pale in colour and the buds will be reluctant to open. However, once its flowers have died, there will be no more because the intensity of light is insufficient for the plant to form more flower buds.

The effects of too much intense sunlight on the African violet may be readily seen. First to be affected are the flowers, and the most sensitive of these are the white blooms. A slight overdose of sun will produce small brown scorch marks on the petals; a heavy overdose of sun will cause the whole flower to turn brown within a few hours. Continued exposure to excessive sun will cause the leaves to be bleached to a pale yellow colour; their growth will tend to be stunted and they will feel hard to the touch. They need urgently to be moved away from this intense light or given some protection. If your only convenient window for growing violets is a sunny one, then in summer the light needs to be filtered. One very successful means of doing this is to make a low curtain about 18in (50cm) high, and fix it across the window behind the sill. Make it from a fairly substantial white fabric (net curtaining is far too thin for this purpose), and you will

'Ballet Silver', a bold and striking bi-colour from Arnold Fischer (Hanover)

> *There are so many disappointed people with healthy-looking violets growing in the corner of the room, on the mantelpiece, on the table, all stoutly refusing to flower. All they need is a little more light, and the windowsill provides the ideal place for growing violets. If your house has no windowsills, then a table standing right in front of the window will suffice. In wintertime, a sunny window is the place for them to be. Winter sun is not strong enough to harm the African violet; indeed, it will help to keep it blooming when everything outside in the garden is drab and drear. Come the spring, the intensity of sunlight will be too strong for the plant to bear, so it should be moved to a window on the shady side of the house.*

find a whole windowsill of violets will be very grateful to you.

All plants tend to grow towards the source of light. This means that the violet will grow towards the window, and unless it is turned regularly, it will become lop-sided. The way to achieve a balanced and symmetrical plant is to turn it frequently, say, once a week, or every time you water it. In that way its growth will be uniform and its appearance enhanced.

Since African violets originate from close to the equator where there is scarcely any 'summer' or 'winter', and where the length of the daylight hours changes very little, the flowering of many plants is triggered by changes in the hours of daylight. For example, chrysanthemums and poinsettias respond to the onset of 'short days' in the autumn by coming into bud. African violets, on the other hand, are not sensitive to changes in the daylight hours and are 'day-length neutral'. Their flowering response depends not on long days or short days, but on the intensity of light. Their flowering season, therefore, is all year round, and they have no need of a rest or dormant period. All of which means that if you get your care conditions right, you can enjoy the beauty of their blossoms in your home every week of the year. No wonder they're so popular!

ARTIFICIAL LIGHT

On Long Island, New York, there is a small commercial African violet nursery without one single greenhouse. The many hundreds of plants produced there are housed in a large, windowless shed, and grow on tiered shelves under fluorescent lights. Under these artificial conditions the whole life-cycle of the African violet from propagation to flowering is achieved, with highly successful results.

This is good news for all those who find themselves short of window space for their plants. No longer are you restricted to finding a suitable location in the home, where it may be that the light coming in at the windows is obscured by a tall building or a large tree. Nor need you worry about how infrequently the sun will shine out from behind the clouds. By the use of artificial light you can create a growing environment for your violets wherever you would like to position them, subject, of course, to meeting their other needs for warmth and freedom from cold draughts. That dark corner in your living-room or the dimly lighted hall can be transformed by the brightness of an indoor flower-bed of colourful African violets.

The type of light source most suitable for this purpose is the fluorescent tube. Indoor light gardens constructed with the use of such tubes are particularly popular among violet-lovers in the United States. These units enable plants to be grown and flowered not only in an otherwise dark corner of the home, but also in a totally windowless basement or attic. Bookshelves and room-dividers are other popular places for growing African violets under lights.

When artificial light is used for growing plants, there are two principal factors to be taken into account: the brightness of the light and the type of light emitted.

The intensity of light is measured by a light-meter calibrated in 'foot-candles' (fc). A series of experiments at the University of Florida into the effect of light intensities on African violets revealed that below 100fc the plants were unable to bloom. As the intensity of light increased, so the growth and flowering of the plants improved. In the

The basis of an indoor light garden is very simple. All you need is a framework to support a twin-lamp fluorescent light unit, complete with its reflectors. If reflectors are not available as part of the unit, then aluminium foil can be used to construct them. All the light produced should be directed in a downward direction on to the plants beneath. A pair of tubes will illuminate a growing area of 12in (30cm) wide and should be so constructed that the light tubes themselves are 8–12in (20–30cm) above the leaves of the African violet. Miniature violets require rather more light and should be raised up on an inverted pot so that they are some 6in (15cm) from the tubes.

Whichever combination of tubes is used, the plants need 12–16 hours' illumination daily. If you are a person of precise habits with an unfailing memory, you may switch the unit on each morning when you get up and switch it off at night when you go to bed. However, it may be a wise move to invest in a time-switch to do the job for you.

Fluorescent light tubes do not last indefinitely, and as they age through use, the light they emit declines in intensity. When grey 'smoke-rings' appear at each end of the tube, it is a sign that the tube needs replacing. Tubes which are used for 12–16 hours each day should be replaced every twelve months. If they are kept beyond that period, your violets will be receiving inadequate light levels, with a negative effect on their growth.

An indoor garden unit enables you to provide optimum light for your violets year-round. If at the same time they are kept in a warm temperature, their growth will accelerate. This means their needs for water and food will also be greater than those growing under natural light, so you should make sure you meet these needs in order that the plants may thrive.

No matter how you construct your indoor garden unit, what better way can there be to brighten up a dull corner than to fill it with light and flowers?

experience of the writer the optimum light intensity is 800fc; below this, flowering is reduced; above this figure, flowers and leaves are at risk of damage through scorching.

Among the varied types of light source available, fluorescent light exhibits the most desirable characteristics for growing plants. It duplicates the light range of the solar spectrum more accurately than other kinds of artificial light; it provides a great deal of light without any damaging heat; and it is economical to use in terms of the amount of light emitted for the amount of electricity consumed.

The most popular lighting arrangement is a combination of two types of fluorescent tube – 'cool-white' and 'warm-white'. One tube of each, in a twin-tube unit, will provide an adequate light source for the growing of African violets. There are special plant-growth tubes available which produce higher levels of the blue and red light which plants use for growing. The light emitted by these lamps appears pinkish-lavender to the human eye and it certainly enhances the appearance of the plants. The leaves look lush and healthy and the colour of the flowers (especially the pinks and reds) is startlingly vibrant. Unfortunately, this appearance is only cosmetic for, on removing the plants from this light into natural daylight, they lose their shimmering glow. There can be no doubt that the natural beauty of the violet is enhanced by these special lights, but the general experience of growers is that a combination of warm–white and cool-white tubes produces equally satisfactory results. Since these latter are universally available and cost considerably less than the special tubes, their use is generally recommended.

Temperatures

The wild ancestors of the cultivated African violets grow in the woods and forests of north–east Tanzania, where they appear to thrive in a very wide band of temperatures. Depending on the altitude at which they are growing, the temperature range they encounter goes from 40 to 80°F (5 to 26°C). Those *Saintpaulia* species which grow at high altitude are best adapted to survive the lowest night-time temperatures, while those from the foothills are happier at the top end of the scale.

If you were to try to grow African violets in a temperature which fell to as low as 40°F (5°C), you would almost certainly meet with disaster. It seems that most modern hybrids trace their ancestry back to the wild ones from the lower slopes of the Usambaras and not to those from the cooler heights. Certainly this can be clearly demonstrated by the trailing varieties, which owe their growth characteristics to *Saintpaulia grotei*, a lowland species. When cold temperatures strike a violet collection, the trailers are the first to collapse.

The *Saintpaulia* species, growing at varying altitudes just south of the equator, are essentially plants of the tropics. In order to survive they need a temperature no lower than 40°F (5°C); so that they may thrive they need ideally a temperature band of 65–75°F (18–24°C). While they will not complain if the thermometer rises to 80°F (26°C) and above, if it drops anywhere near freezing point, then they will collapse. If drowning represents the first great threat to the African violet, then the second threat is represented by freezing temperatures which will kill off any violet which is exposed to them.

In the event of your African violet being faced with very low temperatures, there are two precautionary steps you may take. Experience shows that these plants are much better able to withstand cold weather for a limited period if they are kept on the dry side. Their chances of survival are also considerably enhanced if they are gradually acclimatised to cooler conditions. In an experiment at the African Violet Centre, a batch of plants was acclimatised over a period of weeks to cold temperatures. The experiment was conducted in the early winter in an unheated greenhouse. As the nights became progressively colder, the plants stood up well to the test and no damage was observed until the temperature fell to 37°F (3°C). It should be pointed out that the compost in the pots was kept very dry. Even so, when freezing point was reached at 32°F (0°C), all the plants collapsed.

PLANTS IN THE HOME

What does all this mean for the violets growing in your home? They seem to flourish best in a warm kitchen or living-room. If your home is centrally-heated throughout, then any room should be satisfactory from the point of view of warmth. A simple test of the correct temperature for African violets is to ask yourself if you are feeling warm and comfortable. So long as the answer is 'Yes', then the violets will be comfortable too.

Most people switch off their heating system at night when they go to bed, so there is a period of about eight hours without heat. Surprisingly, the temperature does not fall off too dramatically, especially if the house is well insulated. It may drop to 55–60°F (12–15°C), but a violet can quite easily take this in its stride. As was explained in the earlier section on 'Light', a windowsill is the ideal growing position. However, if you draw the curtains at night, the plants ought not to be left on the windowsill during cold weather. Unless you have double-glazing, the air between the curtain and the window can become very cold indeed during winter. African violets that are trapped there between the frosty glass and the curtain can be very easily chilled, often fatally. The safest policy is to bring the plants away from the window and into the room for the night before drawing the curtains across, returning them to the windowsill in the morning. This wintertime ritual may not be necessary if your windows are double-glazed.

TEMPERATURE TOO HIGH

Continuous high temperatures of 80–90°F (26–32°C) or above are unsatisfactory for African violets. The effects will be evident in a loss of vigour, poor or even nil growth, and a readiness to wilt. At high temperatures, rapid transpiration (that is, the giving off of moisture by the leaves) puts a great deal of stress on the plant, which must pump sufficient water up from the roots to replace that which is being given off.

Usually the plant is unable to cope with the demand and insufficient water reaches the foliage, causing the whole plant to wilt. The persistence of these conditions can result in the death of the plant.

Too high temperatures will also affect the flowers. First, the plant's ability to produce flowers will be impaired; secondly, the size of the blooms will be much smaller than normal; and thirdly, you may well find the flowers dropping off or shrivelling up after a few days.

Continuous high temperatures can also affect the compost. Many proprietary compost formulations contain fertilisers designed to release their nutrients over a period of, say, five months. There will be a fast-release content to provide food for the first ten weeks, and then a slow-release element to keep the supply of food going for the period following on. Unusually high temperatures may cause both slow-release and fast-release fertilisers to discharge their nutrients all at once. Imagine the hottest chilli or curry you've ever eaten and then being forced to eat one at double that strength. Now you may appreciate the predicament of the violet being force-fed at one sitting with half a year's nutrients. The effects are not usually fatal, but all the new, tender young shoots in the crown of the plant will be scorched. The damage looks as though the tips and edges of the shoots have been burned – and so they have, not by fire, but by a chemical overdose.

TEMPERATURE TOO LOW

As the temperature progressively falls, so the growth of the African violet slows down. When a temperature of 50°F (10°C) is reached, then growth will cease entirely. At this point the plant is marking time. Remember that as a plant of the tropics, the *Saintpaulia* is not accustomed to a period of winter dormancy. It is programmed by its inherited genes for continuous growth in warm conditions; to be halted in this growth by prolonged exposure to cool temperatures will put the plant under stress. In its native surroundings the only check to its growth is the occasional drought. With its thick fleshy leaves, holding considerable reserves of moisture, it is well equipped to withstand several weeks of drought.

Prolonged periods of cool temperatures present a hazard it is not equipped to deal with. Growth will be very slow; leaves will become very stiff and will curl down over the edge of the pot; few flowers if any will be produced. Below 50°F (10°C) growth will stop. This is the point at which the plant is most at risk. It is a sitting target for infection and disease, particularly if the compost is wet. It is under great stress, fighting for survival, and a prey to whatever fungal infections are lurking about. Details of these perils are set out in the following chapter, but the most important remedy is to raise the temperature above 60°F (15°C).

> *Your African violets may be spending the winter in a warm living-room, and you may feel confident that no harm can befall them there. Yet there may be hidden hazards even in the warmest room: cold draughts of freezing air squeezing through the window frame, or a chilling down-draught simply coming off the cold glass of the window. Should any leaves be touching the glass during frosty weather, they are likely to be permanently scarred.*

Jack Frost is an insidious enemy whose attacks are not immediately apparent. The effects of a sudden chilling on an otherwise healthy plant are not usually visible straight away. Imagine that you inadvertently left a violet on a windowsill, trapped between the curtain and the glass, and that night there was a severe frost. When you draw the curtain in the morning you realise with alarm what has happened, but the violet looks all right and you sigh with relief at a lucky escape. Not so fast! Later in the day, if you looked closely at the leaves, you would detect a darkening around the leaf-margins with a hazy discolouration over the entire leaf surface. By the next morning the flowers would be hanging their heads and those leaf-margins would have become soft to the touch. The full effects of the chill will not be apparent until thirty-six or forty-eight hours after the event, by which time the plant will be in a state of total collapse. The flower stalks will have fallen over; leaf stalks also will have lost their strength and have collapsed, draping their soft, limp leaves over the side of the pot. Such a disastrous sight is enough to sadden the heart of any plant-lover, filling them with feelings of guilt and remorse.

All may not be lost, however. There is still a slim chance of recovery if the plant is moved into a really warm (68°F/20°C) place. On no account should any water be given until it shows clear signs of recovery. Then, following the golden rule, give no water until the compost has dried right out. If luck is on your side and the plant responds to your first aid, it may be saved, although it will certainly suffer considerable damage. With patience and care fresh new growth will replace the damaged leaves, and after a few months it will once again be a picture of health.

GREENHOUSES AND AFRICAN VIOLETS

It is the writer's experience that small garden greenhouses and African violets do not go well together. The average small greenhouse in Britain is used to produce bedding-out plants in the spring and tomatoes in the summer; it is usually equipped with a small heater to keep it frost-free. The conditions in such a greenhouse are unsuitable for the *Saintpaulia*, being too bright and sunny in summer, and too cold at night and in the winter. Tomatoes and African violets do not mix because they require greatly differing conditions. For example, the bright, unshaded sunlight enjoyed by tomatoes would very swiftly scorch an African violet; while the shady warmth the violet needs would result in a spindly tomato plant climbing to the roof.

Now of course, it is possible to grow African violets in a small greenhouse in the garden, but it must be equipped to provide the conditions required. This will mean that it will be suitable for African violets and some tropical houseplants, but unsuitable for anything else. My own first efforts in violet growing were conducted in a greenhouse measuring 6×10ft (2×3m). It was fitted with two-tiered benching each side of the pathway, under which were fluorescent light tubes. In this way violets were grown under artificial lights on the paved floor and on the lower tier, and under natural daylight conditions on the upper tier of benching. Heating was by electric tubular heaters controlled by a thermostat to give a minimum 68°F (20°C). Each bench was edged with timber and lined with polythene, turning it into a watertight trough for ease of watering. Shading paint was applied to the outside of the glass in the summer and removed with the onset of winter.

This rather sophisticated little greenhouse was home to over a thousand African violets at any one time. The auto-timer ensured that the fluorescent lights were giving the plants sixteen hours of artificial light per day, from 6am until 10pm. On dark winter evenings the greenhouse shone in my garden like a beacon, an object of curious and interested comment among the neighbours.

Feeding Your Plants

The role of fertiliser in improving the growth of plants has been known for at least three thousand years. The ancient Greeks and Romans are recorded as being aware of the benefits of applying animal manure to improve their crops. They used naturally occurring organic material to increase the yield of the crops which they farmed. Today's scientific approach enables us to analyse these organic fertilisers to determine the chemicals they release and match them to the known requirements of various plants under cultivation. Thus we can arrive at a balanced chemical formula which will provide us with a suitable fertiliser for African violets.

All plants need an adequate food supply if they are to thrive. The African violet is no exception and, given the right balance of plant nutrients, will reward its owner with glossy green leaves and sparkling blooms. Violets in top condition do have a gloss about their shiny leaves and their flowers have a sheen which sparkles when caught by the light. Such plants have an aura of good health which depends not only on their growing conditions, but also on their diet.

WHY FEED?

You might be surprised at the number of folk who *never* feed their plants and then complain because they do not thrive. Regular feeding with a suitable plant food is essential for health. Why should such feeding be necessary? The plant nutrients present in the potting compost last for only a limited period of time. Some are absorbed by the growing plant, others are washed out of the compost each time the plant is watered. Most compost mixtures will support a young violet plant for three to six months on the store of nutrients it contains. After this period the growth and development of the plant will slow down if no supplementary feeding is given. Leaves will lose their strong green colour and take on a yellowish shade, and further growth will be hindered. Flowers will be sparse, their petals small and short-lasting. Such a plant, starved of food, will certainly not display glossy green leaves and sparkling blooms. To achieve this it is necessary to replace the nutrients that have been lost or taken up by the plant. This is the role of the plant fertiliser.

TYPE OF FERTILISER

Having established that supplementary feeding is necessary, what should be used and how should it be applied? In any case, what are the particular food requirements of the *Saintpaulia*?

Among the nutrients needed for plant growth, three in particular are of outstanding importance: nitrogen (N), phosphorus (P) and potassium (K). Other nutrients are needed in small or even minute amounts, and in any balanced commercial fertiliser these are always present. Where fertilisers do differ considerably is in the relative quantities of N, P and K. A commercial plant food bottle or packet will have a list of ingredients. It will also usually give the balance of NPK in numbers which represent percentages of the whole. For example, 20-20-20 means that the product contains 20 per cent each of nitrogen, phosphorus and potassium. In other words, this formula shows that these three elements are

46

present in equal quantities.

So far as feeding is concerned, pot plants may be divided into two main groups. In the first group are the foliage plants, also known as 'green' plants because they are grown principally for the beauty of their leaves. Examples of such plants would be *Ficus elastica* (rubber plant), *Monstera deliciosa* (Swiss cheese plant) and *Tradescantia* (Wandering Jew). Fertilisers formulated for these foliage plants are generally high in nitrogen for the promotion of vigorous leaf growth and a rich green colour. A fertiliser best suited to them would have a formula indicating high nitrogen, for example, 30-10-10.

The second group of pot plants are those grown for the beauty of their flowers. This group includes cyclamen, pot chrysanthemum, streptocarpus and, of course, African violet. If these plants are fed with a fertiliser high in nitrogen vigorous leaf growth will be promoted at the cost of poor flowering performance. What is required is a fertiliser which will support leaf growth, but also promote flowering. Such plant foods are usually high in phosphorus or potassium (potash) or both, but they contain sufficient nitrogen to maintain a balance. After all, the nitrogen will play a large part in the growth of the young plant, which is purely vegetative. Only when it approaches maturity will it benefit from an extra boost of P and K to impress you with its blooms.

FIVE WAYS TO FEED YOUR PLANTS

In the shops and garden centres there is a wide range of commercial fertilisers on sale; any one of them will benefit your plants and will be better than not feeding at all. The choice is bewildering, not only of proprietary brands, but also of methods of application. The various formulations are available as liquid, soluble powder or granules, tablets, sticks and mats. By the time you read this the list may be even larger. All are designed to supply the plant with the nutrients it needs for healthy growth; some may also be used for foliar feeding (more about this method later).

A DIET FOR AFRICAN VIOLETS

The kind of formulation needed in an African violet feed is one which is designed for flowering plants. It will contain a balance of food designed to keep leaves green, roots healthy and flower buds coming. The NPK formula for such a fertiliser might read 10-20-20. However, even plant scientists do not have a complete blueprint to predict the detailed effects of these elements and their interaction on each other within the growing plant. In the final analysis it is not the predicted effects which count, but the results. This will perhaps help to explain why there are so many fertilisers with widely differing NPK ratios offered for the same group of plants. For example, many violet enthusiasts swear by a special African violet fertiliser with the NPK formula 12-36-14 (Chempak). Other growers, no less experienced, produce equally good results with a general fertiliser with NPK of 8-11-23 (Phostrogen Phostabs). All that can be said with confidence is that once you have discovered, by trial and error, the brand of fertiliser which gives best results in your own particular growing conditions, then you are well on the way to successful violet growing.

The method of application you elect to use is largely a matter of personal preference. In any event, the manufacturer's instructions should always be carefully read and observed. It would be unwise ever to exceed the recommended strength of dilution. In fact, many violet enthusiasts find that a half-strength dilution produces better results. Feeding is very much a case of individual trial and error, both as to dilution rate and frequency of application. In this area of growing plants there is no substitute for personal experience. At the end of the day it is results that count.

Of the five feeding methods listed above, the two most widely used are liquid fertilisers and powder or granule formulations. Both should be mixed with tepid water at the recommended rate or at a lower strength. They should not be applied to a plant whose compost is completely dry, as this can cause serious damage to the delicate root hairs. If you have allowed your violet to wilt with drought, then just moisten the compost with plain tepid water before administering the fertiliser. This may be poured carefully on to the surface of the compost. Use a small watering can with a long, narrow spout, and take care not to wet the leaves or splash liquid into the crown of the plant. Alternatively, you may stand the plant in a bowl of water to which the feed has been added.

There are many violet-growers who find it beneficial to feed their plants at each watering, using a fertiliser at one half or even one quarter the recommended rate. At such a week dilution it is safe to be lazy and plunge the dry violet straight into a bowl of very dilute feed; no harm should result from this treatment.

Fertilisers which are produced in the form of tablets and sticks depend upon the moisture in the compost for the release of their nutrients. They should be inserted into compost which is already moist, then they can set about doing the job for which they were designed. If you insert them into dry compost, no harm will come to the plant. Neither will there be any benefit because until moisture is present the tablet or stick remains inert and inactive. Give the pot a good soak in water and the nutrients will be released and get to work on your plant.

There are two principal advantages in using fertilisers in tablet or stick form. First, there is no measuring to be done as the tablet or stick is in itself the measured dose. Unless you insert them too frequently, there is little chance of over-dosing the plant. Secondly, once inserted into the compost, the nutrients are located precisely where the plant needs them, which is at its roots. Whereas applications of liquid fertiliser rapidly leach out of the pot, the tablet or stick remains there, releasing its nutrients slowly over a period of weeks.

Four ways of feeding African violets and other pot plants have been discussed: liquid, powder or granules, tablets and sticks. A fifth method is the use of fertiliser mats whereby the plant pot stands on a mat in its saucer or dish. When water is poured into the saucer, the mat becomes saturated and releases its nutrients. These are carried up into the compost by the capillary action of the water. Since many people do water their plants in this way, the mat would appear to be an effective and labour-saving means of ensuring that their plants are fed. With this method it is important to keep topping up the saucer until all the compost in the pot is moist. If this is not done, there will be a build-up of fertiliser in the bottom layer of compost which could prove toxic to the roots.

FOLIAR FEEDING

There is yet another method of feeding plants, one which bypasses the roots and goes directly to the leaves. This is the method known as foliar feeding and is based on the ability of a plant to absorb nutrients directly through the leaf surface. This method has been used successfully with African violets, although more by way of a 'pick-me-up' than as a regular method of feeding. It is not a substitute for root-feeding, but if roots are damaged this can be a useful method of first aid until they have recovered. Also, if a plant has been starved of fertiliser for a long period, this will help to restore it to vigour, and also give it a healthy colour. If you wish to try foliar feeding, it is worth conducting an experiment with one or two sickly violets whose starving leaves have taken on a yellowish appearance.

The method is as follows: from one of the liquid, powder or granule formulations prepare a solution, diluted with *warm* water. Use a brand which claims to be suitable for foliar feeding and dilute according to the recommended rate. Apply the fertiliser solution with a hand mister, making sure that the upper surface of the leaves is well sprayed. Leave the

'Rococo Pink', a popular pink double with 'girl-type' foliage

'Maria', the most successful of the author's 'Frilly' series

plant to dry off in a warm place, out of direct sunlight. This treatment may be repeated at fourteen-day intervals. If the sickly plant responds and its yellowing leaves return to a healthy green, then your experiment will have been a success.

There can be one cosmetically unfortunate side-effect of foliar feeding African violets. As the fertiliser solution dries off on the leaf, it may leave behind a powdery deposit. In the writer's experience this has occurred with a water-soluble powder formulation. This is no great problem on green houseplants with a shiny leaf, since it can easily be wiped off. The hairy leaves of the *Saintpaulia*, however, make removal of this unsightly grey-white stain almost impossible. What is even worse is that the deposit gives the plant the appearance of having a serious attack of powdery mildew.

WHEN TO FEED

In their native tropics where summer lasts all year round, African violets grow steadily throughout the year. They have no natural period of dormancy. However, the violets grown in our homes in more northerly or southerly latitudes, in temperate climates, do suffer a change in their growth pattern. This is caused not by any change in temperature, for our warm homes insulate them from the cold outside; it is caused instead by poor light. Our short winter days, with their low light intensities, slow the growth of African violets very significantly.

What has this to do with feeding them? A vigorously growing violet is using up its supplies of nutrients far more quickly than one which is growing slowly. It follows therefore that in spring, summer and autumn, when the plant is actively growing, it will need regular feeding. During

---

'Pip Squeek', a tiny micro-violet, the smallest in the world, hybridised at Dolgeville, New York, by Lyndon Lyon

'Sprite', one of the attractive little micro-violets raised by the author

winter, growth is slow and feeding should be reduced to a minimum or omitted altogether. Experience indicates that a regular monthly feed from March to October (in the southern hemisphere, September to April) will meet the needs of a strongly growing violet. If you are using tablets or fertiliser sticks, one application every two months would be about right. The nutrients from these sources are released over a period of weeks, unlike liquid applications which are soon washed out of the compost.

During the four midwinter months, feeding will scarcely be required. If you should see signs of yellowing of the leaf, then it would be wise to give a dilute feed. Otherwise, wait until spring comes. Should you be growing violets under artificial lights, then winter growth will be much more active and nutrient needs greater.

TOO MUCH FERTILISER

Fertiliser manufacturers may well recommend a greater frequency of feeding, but since they are in business to sell as much of their product as possible, this is not surprising. Do beware of over-feeding because African violets have a fairly small appetite. They can, in fact, survive for months with no food at all, so allow them as much as they can use without giving them an overdose.

If too much fertiliser is applied to the soil, more than the plant can use, then some of the excess will accumulate. Violets are very sensitive to the fertiliser level in the compost; too great a concentration will seriously damage their delicate and sensitive root hairs. If this condition is not identified and treated, whole sections of root may die, poisoned by too high a concentration of fertiliser. As the roots begin to die, so the top growth of the plant will suffer. The lower, older leaves will begin to rot and drop off; eventually, if it remains untreated the entire plant will wilt and die.

The treatment is simple: to leach a considerable volume of plain warm water through the compost. Pour it on to the surface of the compost. As it runs through the soil and out of the drainage holes at the bottom, it will carry with it the excess fertiliser. This water should not be re-used. If the damage to the root system has not been too great, then with luck you may save the plant and in time restore it to its former beauty.

3
Pests and Diseases

To bring home a beautiful new African violet, only to find after a few weeks that it has fallen victim to some pest or disease, is a very disappointing experience. Pride is replaced with sorrow and anxiety as we weigh up the significance of the attack, wonder about treatment and speculate on the plant's chances of recovery. In this chapter we shall examine the hazards of pest and disease which challenge the violet grower and the ways in which they may be defeated.

All hostile attacks on your plants begin in a very small way: two or three tiny insects, or a small and inconspicuous patch of powdery mildew. If you can spot and identify a threat in its early stages, then your chances of defeating it are very much increased. The watch-word here is 'vigilance'. It may seem to be stating the obvious, but if, like the present writer, you normally wear glasses for reading, then your motto must be 'vigilance with specs on'. It is quite remarkable how easy it is to fail to notice a heavy infestation of tiny aphids. Every time you water your violets, you should give them a close examination. Each plant should be lifted up and turned around in the hand; anything amiss will then be detected early, before it has a chance to get established. This is also a good opportunity to tidy up your plants, removing dead flowers, old flower stalks and leaves. Not only will the plant's appearance be improved, but you will also reduce the chance of infection spreading to the plant from decaying vegetation. Good plant hygiene is an important contribution to the general health of your plants.

It is a good idea to establish this examination routine on a regular basis. In this way you will very soon develop an awareness of the well-being of your plants, their 'aura' of good health. Very often the first sign of trouble with a plant is when this 'good health aura' is suddenly absent. As plant-lovers, an intuitive 'sixth sense' is developed, and it is this rapport with the plant which alerts us when all is not well. This is the time to look very carefully for the cause of the trouble.

IDENTIFYING THE PROBLEM

When a plant looks unhealthy, the cause may be an insect or mite, or an infectious disease. However, it should be pointed out that 90 per cent of premature deaths in African violets are caused not by pest or disease, but improper care. The first task, therefore, is to establish that the trouble is not physiological, that is to say, not caused by over-watering or under-watering, too much light or insufficient light, temperatures too hot or too cold, and so on. This is where good eyesight is so important in being able to see unwelcome visitors, or the start of an alien infection. A great amount of time can be saved in diagnosing the sickness if you are able to see the cause of the problem. If you are satisfied that owner error is not the cause of the problem, then you must suspect an attack from an external source.

Mite and Insect Pests

How often have you admired a beautiful plant in a friend's house, only to find in close-up that it is playing host to some nasty creepy-crawlies? When such an experience occurs in your own home, just as you are proudly showing off your violets to a visitor, it can be somewhat embarrassing. Waiting in the wings there is a whole host of creatures for whom your plants represent breakfast, lunch and dinner for weeks ahead. This army of pests is divided into companies, and each company will attack a different part of the plant.

The roots of the African violet are targeted by nematodes and mealy bugs; their leaves represent grazing meadows for herds of tiny aphids (greenfly); leaf stalks are the particular favourite of scale insects; while flowers risk assault from broad mite, thrips and earwig. But the worst enemy of all creates havoc in the crown of the plant among the newly forming shoots and buds. He is a microscopic mite, called the tarsonemid (or cyclamen) mite.

As you will see, the list of would-be attackers is long; the potential for disaster is alarming. In practice, though, your plants may be free of pests for many months. When these enemies do attack, it is normally one type of insect at a time, which makes your defensive strategy somewhat easier. There is, however, one pest against which African violets in the home have little protection, so we shall look first at enemy number one.

TARSONEMID MITE (CYCLAMEN MITE)
This dreaded mite is too small to be seen with the naked eye, which makes its activities seem secretive and sinister. By the time its presence becomes apparent, it is too late to save the plant. Not only is the violet identified as under attack doomed, but so also in all probability are the other violets in the collection, for if one plant is infested, you can be fairly sure that your other violets are playing host to smaller colonies. Since this mite is too small to be seen with the naked eye, you must learn to identify it from the results of its destructive activity.

Tarsonemid mite favours the very heart of the African violet, the crown of the plant where the new shoots and buds are forming. Once this pest has become thoroughly well established, it is there in the centre of the plant where the tiny new leaves do not appear to grow that its presence becomes evident. The leaves become stiff and brittle and seem to be more hairy than normal, with a greyish colour. Sometimes the stunted centre leaves exhibit a yellow appearance. In the final stage of an attack, the entire centre crown of the plant will be destroyed, leaving not one single growing shoot. Any flower stems that are produced will carry blind buds, or streaked and distorted flowers. This results from the damage caused by the mite during the bud initiation stage in the growing tip of the crown.

Tarsonemid mite is, unfortunately, immune to the effects of regular insecticides. In the commercial production of the *Saintpaulia* an agricultural pesticide called 'Temik' is sometimes used, as its systemic action is very effective against mites. However, this is a highly poisonous material entirely unsuitable for use in the home. The writer is aware of only one effective pesticide which may be used in the home against tarsonemid mite. The name of the product is 'Kelthane' (also known as 'Dicofol') and it is generally available in the United States. Follow the manufacturer's instructions about dilution and spray the plant all over, making sure all leaf surfaces (top and underside) are wet. Kelthane is a contact pesticide, so it only works directly on the body of the mite. Because these creatures are feeding right down in the centre of the plant, they are hidden by leaves and stems. They are also protected by the hairs on the leaves, so make quite sure that the Kelthane penetrates through to where the enemy is hiding. The treatment should be repeated at weekly intervals for a period of five weeks. This will not in any way repair the damage already caused by the mite, but it will allow new young growth to occur.

For those who are unable to obtain a supply of Kelthane, the only responsible course of action is to destroy all affected plants. The entire plant, in its pot, should be either burned or sealed in a refuse sack and disposed of with the household rubbish. On no account should the pot or compost be re-used, neither should an infested plant be thrown out on to the garden. Tarsonemid mite will also make itself at home on other plants, strawberries being among their favourites.

If you have a collection of violets the chances are that if one plant is infested, the other plants in the house will be in the process of being colonised by the little beasts. Examine all your plants very carefully, and if you detect any suspicious-looking symptoms, dispose of the plants as above. The best long-term advice is, 'If in doubt, throw them out.' There are experienced violet enthusiasts who recommend that if one mite-infested plant is identified, the entire collection should be destroyed. All trays and shelves on which plants have been growing should be wiped down with a strong solution of domestic bleach, and then washed with plain hot water. It is also recommend that no new African violets should be brought into the house for a period of three months. By this time the hidden mites not killed by the bleach will hopefully have died of old age or starvation.

BROAD MITE
The broad mite is of a similar microscopic size to its cousin the tarsonemid mite; but whereas the latter favours the crown of the plant, the broad mite prefers to feed on young leaves and flowers. The first sign of broad mite attack is a mottled or faded appearance of the flower petals, almost as if they had powdery mildew. The leaves of the violet may seem lack-lustre. Young leaves in the centre of the plant will have an unnatural shiny, silvery appearance. They will seem to be rather elongated, curling down at the tips. Tarsonemid mite is slow moving, content to remain in the crown of the plant; broad mite is fleet of foot and travels freely over the plant, or the plant next to it. Thus it will very quickly spread to other violets in the vicinity.

Treatment of a plant with broad mite is the same as that for the tarsonemid. If Kelthane is used, even greater care should be taken to wet the undersides of leaves and the flower heads, since this mite may be found all over the plant. In the absence of Kelthane or any other effective miticide, the plants must be carefully destroyed.

The old dictum, 'Prevention is better than cure', was never more true than in the case of mite infestation. One risk which you cannot guard against is that these unwelcome visitors will arrive on the air, blown by the wind and entering your home through an open window. If you value fresh air for yourself and your plants, that is one risk you have to take. It seems, however, that most pests are carried into the home not on the air, but on the leaves and flowers of newly purchased pot plants. They may come from a very reputable source, but even so they may be host to some unwanted guests. The wise thing to do is to place them in quarantine. In order to safeguard your collection of violets and other plants, newcomers should be quarantined for at least six weeks. Keep them well away from your other plants, in a separate room if possible. Always tend your established plants before the new arrivals; use a second watering-can for the quarantined plants, and always thoroughly wash your hands after treating them.

Mites not only attack the *Saintpaulia* and other members of the Gesneriad family, but they will also travel into your home on begonias and cyclamen. In fact, any plant or even cut flowers can be a mite carrier. It only takes one or two mites to start a disastrous infestation, so safeguard your collection by putting every newcomer into quarantine.

RED SPIDER MITE

The red spider mite is probably the most common of this family of plant-eating mites. It is easily identified because it actually spins a web on the underside of the leaves of its host plant. Several writers treat it as a pest of African violets; however, the present writer has yet to come across a case of red spider mite infestation, despite having grown millions of violets over many years. I recall with shame one greenhouse of violets with under-bench weeds riddled with red spider mite, yet not one violet was infested. Even when the weeds were killed, the mites did not migrate to the violets on the benches. It seems, therefore, that they dislike African violets and will not attack them. So there at last is one piece of good news about mites!

APHIDS (GREENFLY)

There are a great many aphid species, only a few of which attack African violets. Those which do attack the plants are very small indeed, and since they are usually green in colour, can easily escape detection. Often the first sign that you have aphid trouble is the appearance of tiny white specks on the leaves of the plant. Although they look like white insects and are frequently but mistakenly thought to be whitefly, they are in fact the cast skins of the aphids. Whitefly appear to dislike African violets and will not feed on them.

The tiny aphids which feed on the flowers or leaves of African violets multiply rapidly by reason of their short but unusual life-cycle. These aphids are all unmated wingless females which are able to produce all-female wingless broods. However, if the infestation becomes very heavy and the food source becomes scarce, a few winged females and winged males are born. These fly to another area, mate and lay eggs, which after some time hatch into wingless females. Thus the cycle is repeated. These late-hatching eggs can catch you out, for just when you think the infestation has been eradicated, they can reappear as if by magic.

The commonest aphid on violets is the green species, difficult to see because it has a natural camouflage as it feeds on the green leaves. Only as it grows fat by feeding on your

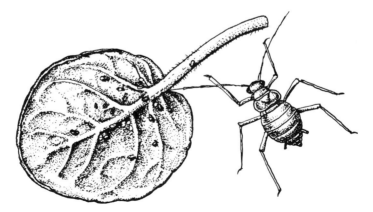

Aphids will feed on both flowers and leaves of the African violet

plants and sheds its skin, does it begin to reveal itself. The white specks of the cast skins are clearly visible on the leaves. These aphids also exude a honeydew which causes a stickiness on the lower leaves and around the tray or shelf on which the plant is standing. With time, a black fungal mould will grow on the sticky honeydew and be clearly visible as a grey/black patch.

Once you have identified this pest, the remedy is to select one of the many insecticides, both systemic and contact, which will destroy aphids. Also available are specific aphid insecticides which are selective in their action, killing only aphids and harmless to beneficial insects. One such specific aphicide is ICI Abol G, containing pirimicarb. These chemicals are contact insecticides and only work if in direct contact with the body of the pest. They are used as a spray or drench on the foliage at the first signs of aphid attack. Other contact insecticides, such as those containing malathion, resmethrin and the pyrethrums, may also be used. These are all broad spectrum formulations which will kill many different insects, and are also applied as a spray or drench for foliage.

In addition to the contact insecticides, there are the so-called 'systemic' insecticides. These formulations poison the aphids by way of the sap of the host plant. Applied to the compost, the insecticide is taken up by the roots of the plant and distributed by the sap throughout the whole of the foliage. Thus, any insect feeding anywhere on the plant, even in the most hidden places, will poison itself as it feeds. This thorough-going action of the systemic insecticides is a great advantage, as is also the preventive action of the residual chemical remaining for some weeks in the plant cells. Aphids hidden inside tight buds or shoots may escape if protected from the contact insecticides; but wherever they feed, they will be poisoned by the action of the systemic pesticide.

If you are alarmed at the idea of using these poisonous chemicals, there is a safe, but less effective, remedy. You may invert the plant and immerse the foliage in a weak solution of soapy or detergent water, taking care to keep the compost above the water level. This will hopefully wash off some, if not all, the aphids, but is likely to leave the immature insects on the plant. Regular repetition of this procedure would therefore appear to be necessary.

General good hygiene and the quarantining of new plants offer the best hopes of prevention. This cannot be guaranteed, though, as any plant from outside, even cut flowers, can carry aphids. They may be carried indoors on clothing, or even, as with the mites, blown in on the wind through an open window. At least you know that if you get an infestation of this pest, your chemical armoury will enable you quite easily to kill it stone dead.

THRIPS

African violets are grown principally for the beauty of their flowers. Any pest which attacks this most attractive feature of the plant has to be a leading candidate in the unpopularity stakes. Not only do thrips attack flowers, but they also do a disproportionate amount of damage in ratio to their numbers. Because they are so tiny, the first indication of their presence is the damage they cause. They are sucking insects which attack flower petals and leaves; they will also chew holes in the pollen sacs, causing the pollen to spill out on to the petals. Thrip-infested blossoms will appear speckled or mottled, while damaged leaves will be similarly marked, showing white against the green of the undamaged areas. Leaves may be so seriously affected by the feeding activity of thrips that they will collapse, the leaf blade and stalk turning black. Unless this dead material is removed, botrytis fungus may set in and spread quickly, killing the entire plant.

Immature thrips are creamy-yellow in colour; on reaching adulthood they turn dark brown or black, and develop wings. They may be treated successfully with a number of insecticides, both contact and systemic; check the label for the list of pests controlled.

Just when you think that you have mastered nature's pest problems, a resistant strain appears, and so it is at the time of writing with thrips. A race of thrips immune to all our prescnt-day insecticides has appeared and is known as 'western flower thrips'. It is posing a severe threat to commercial flower growers and is particularly fond of chrysanthemum and Gesneriads (including African violets and streptocarpus). Fortunately, science is not far behind, and a new insecticide which will control even this resistant strain is soon to be available. It will probably be too toxic for domestic use, however. So if you have an infestation of thrips which are not controlled by treatment with a regular insecticide, you may have the misfortune to have the mutant strain. Should this be the case, all infected plants should be incinerated or sealed in a refuse sack and disposed of in the normal way.

EARWIGS AND MICE

It may seem odd that earwigs and mice should be coupled together in this section on pests. Certainly they make strange bedfellows. However, in their list of favourite gastronomic treats they share a passion for the pollen sacs of African violets. Their discrepancy of size means that their table manners differ. The earwig, as befits its size, is a delicate eater, puncturing the anthers with pin-sized holes to get at the pollen inside. In the process it spills a fair bit on to the petals, and thus gives the game away.

The mouse, being considerably larger, bites off the entire pollen sac. Its appetite for this delicacy is insatiable. One small mouse will, in the course of a night, work through thirty or forty African violet plants on a greenhouse bench. You may imagine the havoc this little pest can cause in a greenhouse full of specimen plants just before a major show!

Both earwigs and mice are night-shift workers and feed at night. You will not catch them, therefore, on the plants during daylight hours. If you suspect earwigs, then you must go round your plants with a torch after dark, and you may be able to catch the culprit in the act. If the damage indicates mouse activity – they normally leave droppings behind – then set a trap. Because the damage they do is perpetrated at night, the cause may remain an unsolved mystery for a long time. Thrips will leave a fine dusting of pollen; earwigs scatter pollen in tiny lumps; mice eat the entire pollen sac. And just in case you ever should need to know, rats eat everything – pollen sacs, pistil, flower petals and stalk. Rats which are really hungry will also eat the leaves.

SCALE INSECTS
These insects rarely feed on African violets, but it is as well to be aware of them. They are small, round, limpet-like creatures which can grow up to ¼in (6mm) long. The shell-like covering provides a protective shelter for the insect as it sucks the juices from the host plant, usually feeding on a

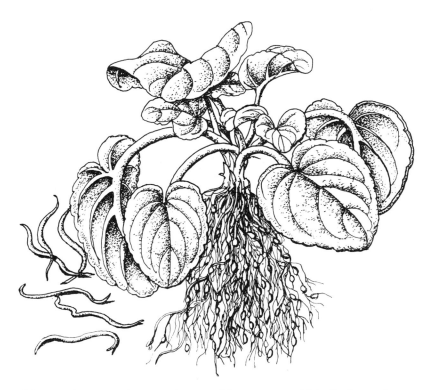

Nematodes are microscopic parasitic worms which feed on plant roots. Their presence is revealed by root-knots, swellings of the root which look like tiny beads

leaf-stalk. Scale insects, like aphids, secrete a sticky honey-dew substance. This in turn may be colonised by a black sooty mould, and you may imagine that a badly infested plant will look pretty nasty.

Young scale insects will crawl slowly around the plant; adults tend to attach themselves very firmly to one place. Normally grey or brown in colour, they are very difficult to dislodge once they have become permanently attached to the plant. It is best to attack these disfiguring pests through the sap on which they are feeding. Use a systemic insecticide recommended for scales, then once the toxic chemical is flowing in the sap, the creatures will poison themselves as they feed. It will then be possible to remove the dead insects from the plant and wash off the deposits of honeydew.

MEALY BUGS
There are two principal races of mealy bug; one feeds above ground on the leaves, the other lives below soil level and feeds on the roots. Both mealy bugs feed on the juices of the

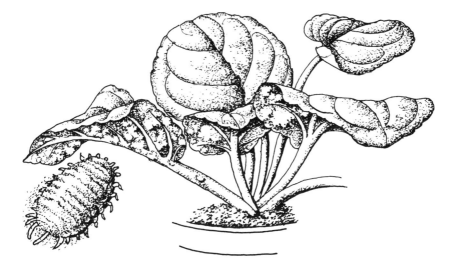

Leaf mealy bugs are coated with a white powdery wax, and feed on the under-surface of the leaf

host plant, and if untreated will cause serious injury and eventually the death of the plant.

Leaf mealy bugs grow up to ¼in (6mm) long and are coated with a white, powdery wax. They prefer to feed on the under-surface of the leaf, or down in the leaf axil. A clear give-away to the presence of mealy bug is the discovery of small cotton masses on the plant, like tiny lumps of cotton wool. In these cotton masses the insect lays its eggs and these should be carefully removed if possible.

The soil mealy bug is also known as the Pritchard mealy bug. They are creamy white in colour and resemble tiny grains of rice, measuring only ¹⁄₁₆in (1.5mm) long. They feed on the small root hairs of the plant, and unchecked can cause great damage to these new roots. A plant suffering from this pest looks sick and wilted, and has poor vigour. When examining the roots for mealy bug, a magnifying lens is a great advantage since they are so small. The discovery of small cotton wool-like masses among the roots is the clearest sign of an infestation.

Treatment with a systemic insecticide should eliminate both species of this pest. The treatment should be repeated two or three times at ten-day intervals in order that a newly hatching generation does not cause a fresh infestation. To kill the soil mealy bug it may be necessary to drench the compost with a general systemic insecticide; alternatively, a drench of Malathion may be used.

(*top left*) 'Fancy Pants', a most popular bi-colour

(*top right*) 'Harlequin' was raised at the African Violet Centre and made its debut at the Chelsea Flower Show 1987

(*below left*) 'Magic Trail', a free-flowering trailer with a cascade of semi-double pale-pink stars

(*below right*) 'Mini Marina', a micro-violet with girl-type foliage (the author)

VINE WEEVIL

The vine weevil is a rare but determined violet killer. In its larval stage it grows up to ½in long (13mm), with a creamy segmented body and a chestnut-brown head. It has a voracious appetite, living in the soil and feeding on the violet roots. When it has consumed most of the roots, it eats its way up inside the centre of the violet's stem. If you have not discovered the pest by this time, it really is too late. You will find you can lift the plant off the soil because it has no root left to anchor it. Look up inside the stem and there you will find the culprit.

Hopefully, you will have noticed a lot earlier that your plant looked limp and sick, and you may have discovered the grub among the roots before he really started on his vertical journey. The treatment is very simple – knock him out on to the floor and put your foot on him.

ROOT NEMATODES

Root nematodes are microscopic parasitic worms which infest the roots of affected plants. A violet under attack from this pest will assume a sickly yellow-green colour and will have a tired, limp appearance. If you suspect nematodes, knock the plant out of its pot so that you may examine its roots. An infested plant will have root-knots, swellings on the roots which look like small beads; this is definite evidence of the presence of nematodes. These knots prevent the roots supplying the plant with the food and water it needs so that it will slowly starve to death.

The best and safest action to take on identifying nematodes is to destroy and dispose of plant, compost and pot. These parasites are easily transmitted from one plant to another by water (if they stand in a tray together), or by infected compost. The only effective way to kill these pests is by the use of highly toxic chemicals called nematicides, which are

---

'Kristi Marie', a dusky-red beauty from Lyndon Lyon, but a shy bloomer

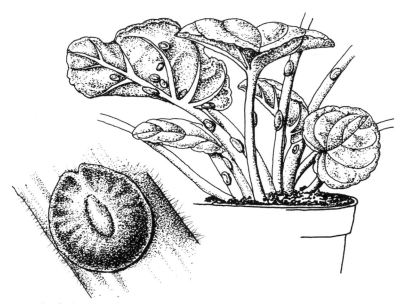

Scale insects feed on the leaf-stalks of the African violet

---

not suitable for use in the home. Fortunately, however, this pest is very rare in African violets and you would be very unlucky to meet it.

SPRINGTAILS
These little insects are about ⅙in (4mm) long and live on the soil surface or in the saucer beneath the pot. They have the ability to jump surprising distances, hence their name of springtails. They do not harm the foliage of African violets, but severe infestations can harm the roots of the plant. Good plant hygiene will help to prevent them; if they do become a nuisance, a soil drench with an insecticide should destroy them.

SCIARID FLY
This is another nuisance pest which, although it does little harm, is not nice to have around your plants. In appearance it is a smaller edition of the fruit fly and black in colour. Unfortunately, it is resistant to a wide range of insecticides.

72

The most effective way to treat this creature is to attack it in the larval stage. Its grubs live in the top ½in (13mm) or so of the soil surface. They are tiny, translucent, worm-like larvae, and they thrive in soil which is kept continuously moist. If you do have a sciarid problem, it usually indicates that you have been keeping the compost too wet.

The most effective treatment is to remove the top ¾in (18mm) of soil from the pot and replace it with fresh

---

PREVENTION

This list of potential pests and parasites represents a real threat to the health and well-being of the African violet. They can, however, be deterred and kept at bay by some very simple and straightforward preventive action.

1 When potting up your plants always use new, unused pots; or, at the very least, if you re-use old pots make sure they have been well scrubbed and sterilised.
2 Always use fresh compost. On no account should old compost be re-used for potting because it may well contain the eggs or larvae of the pests you are fighting against.
3 Always keep your plants clean and tidy. Remove dead flowers and leaves promptly and also any that appear to be diseased.
4 Quarantine all new arrivals; you cannot be certain that they are pest-free, no matter how good a home or nursery they came from.
5 Keep all cut flowers away from your violets. It is so easy for two or three aphids or thrips to drop off the chrysanthemum flowers, for example, on to your violets below and start a fresh colony there.
6 Be prepared should the worst happen and unwelcome visitors appear on your plants. Keep in stock a contact and systemic pesticide so that you can take counter-measures immediately you find you have trouble. These insects and mites multiply so rapidly that there is no time to be lost if they are to be controlled and eliminated.

---

compost. To prevent a further reinfestation, make sure you allow the surface to dry out before giving the plant any water.

Diseases

The infections which attack African violets are caused by organisms belonging to either fungus or virus disease groups. Sometimes they can infect your plant with alarming speed so that a plant which on Sunday was a picture of health, can look a sorry mess on Monday. If you are following good hygiene practices, then the chances of a disease problem are greatly reduced. The isolation of all new African violets, as also of other new plants, is an important rule to follow in this respect. Since fungus and virus organisms are microscopic, it is most important that care is taken to eliminate the chance transference of these organisms from infected to healthy plants. After working on new arrivals, or suspect plants, hands and implements should be thoroughly washed before working on the other plants in your collection.

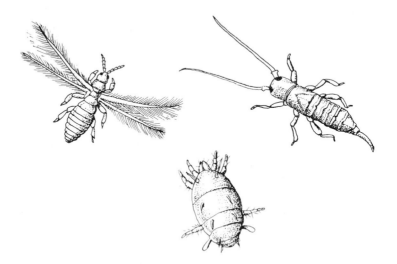

Thrip (left), mite (centre) and springtail

VIRUS DISEASES

These are the most difficult diseases to diagnose on an African violet because most of the symptoms are similar to those caused by insects or mites. Virus infections will cause streaking and deformity of flower and leaf. Otherwise the plant may appear to be in good health, but growth will be abnormal and fewer flowers will be produced. There is no cure for an African violet which has become infected by a virus, so once you have eliminated other possibilities and decided your plant has a virus, it is wise to dispose of it carefully before other plants become infected. Virus infections are spread by mites and aphids, among others. If you keep your plants free of these pests, then you can hope never to have a virus problem.

PHYTOPTHORA

This is the fastest killer among the fungal diseases and is also known as 'Sudden Black Death'. The organism strikes at the very heart of the violet, in the crown, turning it black. This black infection then spreads out along the leaf and flower stalks, causing them to collapse. From the time you spot the tell-tale blackening of the tiny leaves in the crown, until the time the plant collapses, can be as short as twenty-four hours. It is a galloping, fatal infection.

Some years ago a severe outbreak of this disease occurred at the African Violet Centre. It rampaged through the propagation house destroying the young plants by their thousand. The organism is soil-borne, and at that time there was no preparation commercially available that would kill it. By a stroke of good fortune we discovered that the British pharmaceutical company May & Baker were working on a fungicide which it was hoped would be the first to kill the phytopthora pathogen. Hearing of our problem with a crop of *Saintpaulia*, they asked if we would trial the product. Like a drowning man clutching at a straw, we grasped the opportunity with both hands.

The results were remarkable beyond our wildest hopes. We drenched every plant with this new, nameless systemic

75

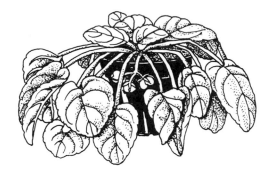

A victim of the 'sudden black death' fungus disease *Phytopthora*

---

fungicide, particularly all newly pricked-out cuttings and freshly potted plants. The treatment stopped the rot in its tracks and halted the epidemic which threatened to overwhelm the business so carefully built up over the years. We lost twenty thousand plants, but saved the business. And to this very day, all our trays of compost are dunked in this fungicide before the young cuttings are pricked out.

The results we achieved helped to persuade May & Baker that this fungicide was worth launching on to the commercial market. It was given the name 'Aliette', and at the time of writing is in widespread commercial use for a wide range of crops. Alas, it is not available to the general public for home use. In any event, once a plant has contracted phytopthora, it is too late to save it. The sooner you shoot it into the refuse sack, the quicker you reduce the chances of the infection spreading.

PYTHIUM

This fungus, like phytopthora, is soil- or compost-borne and is a real plant-killer. It attacks the crown of the plant, the leaves becoming shrivelled and whitish looking. A black rot affects the base of leaf and flower stalks, causing them to fall off the plant. This is quite a distinctive condition, because the leaf stalk and blade remain green, whereas with phytopthora

76

the whole stalk turns a mushy black. Both these diseases are carried by spores which survive in soil or compost until they find a susceptible host plant. The spores may also travel through water to infect adjoining plants standing in the same watering tray.

Pythium is a killer, and once a plant is infected it has little chance of recovery. Rapid disposal of diseased plants will reduce the risk of an epidemic. Most outbreaks of pythium and phytopthora seem to come from infected compost. The use of sterile compost will eliminate this risk; if in doubt about the compost, heat it to 180°F (82°C) for 30 minutes and keep it enclosed before use.

BOTRYTIS

This member of the fungus family occurs always as a secondary infection, colonising plant tissue which has already been affected with rot. It appears as grey, fluffy needles on dead or dying stems and leaves, frequently after a plant has been damaged by insects. By the time botrytis sets in, the plant is probably beyond help. However, it sometimes happens that only isolated leaves are affected and if these are carefully removed, the rest of the plant may be saved. The threat of botrytis is one very good reason why you should be careful over plant hygiene. If dead flowers and decaying leaves are not removed from the plant, then this fungus is being given an open invitation. Botrytis can be controlled by treating with 'Benlate' (benomyl). Unfortunately, this chemical will leave a white deposit on the leaves of African violets which it may prove difficult to remove.

POWDERY MILDEW

This fungal disease will attack a wide range of plants, both indoor and out, including African violets. Its spores are air-borne and infected plants display a white powdery discolour-ation on flowers, stems and leaves. In the writer's experience this infection usually starts on flower buds or flowers and on the stalk just below the flower head. The discolouration is not easily seen and if untreated will cause flowers to be small and deformed, some buds going brown and failing to open. The infection of the neck of the flower stem will eventually cause the flower head to fall over as the disease eats into the tissue. The leaves are next to be infected, with small round patches of fungus. These look as though the lady of the house has spilled some talcum powder on to the plant. If left untreated, the powdery deposit will cover the entire plant, sapping its energy and causing its eventual collapse.

Mildew is most frequently a problem of late spring, when warm days and cold nights encourage its development. Sudden temperature changes, particularly cold draughts in an otherwise warm room, will certainly encourage the disease. Infected buds, flowers and flower stalks should be removed. The plant should be sprayed with 'Nimrod T' (containing bupirmate and triforine) or 'Benlate' (benomyl). Remember when spraying an African violet always to use warm water, and ensure that the plant is not exposed to direct sunlight until the leaves are quite dry.

4
Growing your own
African Violets

African violet growing is fun; it is also very rewarding.
Watching the buds on your plant develop and burst open into
beautiful flowers brings great pleasure. Think how much
greater that satisfaction would be if you had propagated and
raised the plant by yourself. You would experience a deep
and genuine pride in your achievement, and also be the object
of the envy and admiration of your friends.

There are two methods of reproducing the *Saintpaulia*. The
first method is called 'vegetative reproduction' and is the
propagation of plants by means of leaf-cuttings or plant
division. The second method of raising new plants is by
'sexual reproduction', that is, by cross-fertilising the flowers
of two separate plants, resulting in the production of seed
which, when sown, will germinate into new plantlets. This
technique is known as 'hybridising' (see Chapter 5).

In this chapter we shall see how, with a little care and
know-how, a violet collection can be increased by leaf-
cuttings and plant division. Once the propagation techniques

have been mastered, many possibilities will open up. From that old violet of which you are so fond, you will be able to raise healthy young plants. Should you come across a beautiful new violet in the home of a friend, you have only to beg a leaf to be able to grow one for yourself. When you have got into the swing of propagation, you will find that you are not only increasing your collection, but that you are producing more plants than you need or have house room for. These may be used as gifts, to the delight of your friends, or be donated for sale at charity events. Either way you will obtain great personal satisfaction and a real sense of achievement. Among your circle of friends and acquaintances you will gain the reputation of being something of a plant expert. They will soon be asking your advice and the secrets of your success; you would be surprised how many new friendships have been started in this way.

There is nothing difficult about propagating and raising your own plants and no expensive equipment is needed. Anybody with a warm living-room or kitchen can be successful in growing their own violets. There is, however, one attribute which is absolutely necessary in the would-be violet propagator, without which there can be no success – patience. Without the discipline of patience, success will elude you. If you are the kind of person who plants a cutting, only to lift it out the next day to see if it has rooted, then violet propagation is not for you. Mother nature will not be rushed. The time-span from a leaf-cutting to an African violet in bloom can be as long as eighteen months to two years, although under ideal conditions this may be reduced to twelve months. A great deal depends upon the growing conditions, especially the temperature; it is this which largely determines the rate of growth. Briefly, the warmer it is, the quicker they grow; the cooler the temperature, the slower will be the growth.

Leaf-Cuttings

The ability of the African violet to produce from a leaf-cutting an entirely new plant is one of nature's wonders.

Even more remarkable is the way in which, under laboratory conditions, tiny pieces of leaf will produce many plantlets. This technique is called 'micro-propagation' or 'tissue-culture' and is used by commercial growers to produce large numbers of identical plants in a very short space of time. More amazing still, it has been claimed that every single cell of the violet leaf, of which there are hundreds of thousands, has the ability to reproduce itself. By the laboratory technique known as 'cell-culture' one leaf could in theory yield as many as one million plants!

These advanced laboratory techniques, however, play no part in the way in which home-grown violets are raised, but they are all methods of vegetative propagation and they all have this in common, that they generally produce plants which are identical in flower colour and leaf form to their parents. Although this is generally the case, nature is not always that predictable.

You may have heard friends refer to a particular plant as a 'sport' or 'mutation'. It sometimes happens that a plant propagated from a cutting differs significantly from its parents. Such a plant is a freak and is known as a 'sport' or 'mutation'. In the writer's experience, such sports are regular occurrences in the propagation of bi-coloured African violets. A violet with blue-edged white flowers will often sport a percentage of progeny with all-blue flowers and less frequently with all-white flowers. Cultivars with too high a proportion of sporting in propagation are clearly unsuitable for commercial use. This can be very disappointing for both the grower and the violet enthusiast. Some hybrids which are stable in normal leaf propagation, will unexpectedly mutate when put into tissue culture in a laboratory.

This apparently random appearance of freaks and mutations can also be viewed positively as part of the surprising excitement of growing African violets. It was, after all, by a series of unexpected mutations that the wide range of flower colours and plant forms of these plants first began to appear. Even today some new cultivars owe their origin not to the hybridiser, but to the eagle-eyed violet enthusiast who spotted a mutation. So when you begin to propagate your own violets, do not be surprised if a sport appears. It may be even more attractive that its parent plant. If it proves to be itself stable in propagation, then you could be in a position to name and introduce an entirely new and unique African violet.

WILL ANY LEAF DO?

The basic method of taking a leaf-cutting is quite straight-forward. It consists simply of removing a leaf from the plant, inserting the stalk in compost or water and waiting for nature to do the rest. However, experience has proved that if certain procedures are followed, greater success will result. First, which leaf should you choose and will any leaf be suitable? The answer to this question is that the choice of leaf will often determine whether you will succeed or fail.

Any leaf will not, in fact, produce the desired results. The leaf chosen for propagation must be healthy and undamaged, unaffected by pest or disease, and with plenty of growing left to do. Too often folk will taken an old, tired, outside leaf from their plant and expect it to do wonders for them. It is not surprising that they are usually disappointed. Such an old leaf has little vigour remaining, is approaching the end of its life-span, and is certainly a most unsuitable candidate for plantlet production. Such a leaf may, if you are lucky, form roots; but it will lack the energy to produce new shoots. Having established a root system, it may well sit in its pot for a year or more, apparently green and healthy, but doing nothing about sending up new shoots. Many would-be violet propagators have had that experience and wondered where they went wrong.

Which, then, is the correct leaf to choose? There is an old wives' tale that you must use a 'pointed' leaf, not a 'round' one. This story contains not even a grain of truth; the shape of leaf depends upon the particular variety of African violet. Some have pointed leaves, some have rounded ones; either may be used in propagation, with an equal chance of success. If you choose the correct leaf from your plant, you may well be rewarded with not only one plantlet, but as many as ten or more – enough to supply not only your own needs, but also to give away to your friends.

> *The right leaf to choose for propagation is one from the middle band of leaves. Do not use a leaf from the outer ring of old and fully mature leaves; neither should you take a very young one from the centre crown of the plant. Leaves for propagation should be chosen from the middle band of leaves which are now mature, yet still have plenty of growing left to do. These leaves will have just the vigour needed to get on with the job of rooting and shooting.*

TAKING A CUTTING

In order to remove the cuttings from the parent plant it is best to break the leaf stalk away from the heart of the plant. Grasp the selected leaf firmly between thumb and forefinger and give it a sharp sideways tug; with luck, it will break clean away from the stem, leaving very little stalk behind. If you experience difficulty in doing it this way, use a sharp knife to sever the leaf stalk as close to the stem as possible. If possible, avoid leaving a stump of stalk on the stem as this may become diseased as it decays, and spread rot to the stem and centre of the plant. Ensure that the selected parent plant is moist at the roots, with its leaves turgid with sap. In this condition the leaf stalks are quite brittle and easy to snap off or slice through. When the plant is dry, its leaf stalks are rubbery and difficult to break off or slice cleanly through.

Once the leaf-cutting has been removed from the plant, it should be trimmed up before it is planted. The length of stalk available will, of course, depend on how much stalk remains on the leaf when it is removed from the plant. To propagate leaves in compost, 1–1½in (25–38mm) of stem should be left attached to the leaf. For propagation in water, a rather longer stalk will be an advantage. This final trimming is most important not only for reducing the stem to the ideal length, but also, by the angle of the cut, providing the maximum potential area for the formulation of roots. Better rooting

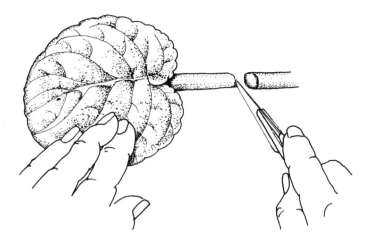

After removing the selected leaf from the plant, trim the stalk with a sharp knife or razor blade

---

action will result if the cut is made at a diagonal angle and not simply straight across the stalk. The reason for this is that a diagonal cut will expose a greater area of stalk core from which the roots will develop.

The final trimming of the stalk may be carried out using a very sharp knife or razor-blade, because a clean slice is essential. Should the trimmed end of the stalk be bruised during the cutting process, then there is a serious risk of infection setting in. If this happens, the leaf, instead of rooting, will rot.

ROOTING IN WATER

There are two methods by which leaf-cuttings may be rooted. The one favoured by commercial growers is rooting in compost (see p90). The other method, popular with many people who grow their violets at home, is to root the leaves in water. This is the procedure to follow: take a glass jar and add water at room temperature until it is three-quarters filled. Tap-water may be used, but rain-water or distilled water may be better. The glass jar may be either clear or coloured. Dark glass will discourage the formation of algae in the water, but will make it difficult for you to watch the development of roots. Clear glass will enable you to see readily how the roots and plantlets are forming, and also enable you to check on the water level.

The violet leaf should be suspended above the water so that the end of the stalk is submerged to a depth of 1in (25mm). The usual method of achieving this is to cover the top of the jar with paper, held in place by a rubber band; alternatively, a piece of aluminium foil may be moulded over the top, or it may be covered with plastic clingfilm. Whichever method of covering the jar is used, one or more holes should be made in the material through which the stalk may be passed. By this

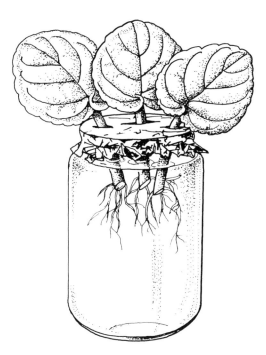

Leaves for rooting in water will require a longer stalk than those of compost-rooting. Cover jar with foil or cling-film and make holes for the insertion of the stalks

means the leaf blade will be supported on the jar cover, while the end of the stalk will be submerged in the water.

If this method of rooting leaves is used, then the cuttings will obviously need to have a fairly long stalk, say, 2–3in (50–75mm). Two or three cuttings may be placed in the same jar; any more would lead to difficulty separating the tangled roots. Despite all precautions, it sometimes happens that a leaf will begin to decay. When this happens the diseased leaf must be removed and disposed of immediately, otherwise it will infect other leaves in the same rooting jar. It would be wise at the same time to replace the water with some which is fresh and uncontaminated with disease organisms, or, better still, use a fresh jar.

Once the leaves have been set up in the jar with their feet comfortably immersed in water, the jar should be placed in a warm room where it will receive plenty of light, although not in direct summer sunlight. Do make sure to label each cutting so that it can be identified later and you will know what colour of flower to expect when it reaches maturity. One way is to stitck a small adhesive label to each leaf, with variety name or simply colour; alternatively, this information may be written on a plastic plant label and attached to the jar by a rubber band. The advantage of this latter method is that when you pot up the leaf into compost, the label can simply be inserted into the pot.

In the early days of space flight, there was one particularly hazardous period which returning astronauts had to face, known as 're-entry'. This was the transition from space flight back to travelling through the earth's atmosphere. There is one particularly hazardous period which water-rooted leaves must overcome, and that is the transition from the medium

---

'Colorado', a tried and tested favourite from Reinhold Holtkamp, used extensively by violet hybridisers

'Silver Milestone Star', a striking sport out of Joan Hill's 'Silver Milestone'

of water to that of compost. This is the time when many well-rooted leaves are lost, to the distress of their erstwhile proud owners. This is also the time when you realise that perhaps that medicine bottle was not such a good idea after all, because the neck is too narrow to draw the roots and plantlets through. Always use a wide-necked jar – the usual jam jar is perfect for the job.

THE TRANSFER TO COMPOST

The chances of successfully transferring the cutting into compost are greater if this is done *before* small plants appear. As soon as the leaf-cutting has produced a sturdy root system, say, after six to eight weeks, it should be removed and potted up. Prepare 3½in (9cm) plastic pots, fill with warm (ie room temperature) peat-based compost. Firm the compost only gently; if it is pressed down too hard, the shy roots of the violet will have difficulty penetrating it. Use a low-nutrient mixture specially formulated for seedlings or cuttings. Using a plant label or a finger, make a hole in the compost and insert the cutting. Water it in from above with water which is just warm to the touch.

Newly potted leaf-cuttings and plantlets experience great stress before they become established. This is caused by the leaves giving off moisture (known as 'transpiration') which the plant is unable to replace because it has no roots. The lack of a root system, or the possession of an inadequate one, means that the cutting is unable to siphon water up from the compost, through its sap channels, and into the leaf. Because the leaf is therefore unable to replace its moisture, it begins to flag and wilt; unless fresh supplies of moisture arrive within a few days, it will die.

'Starry Trail', with its unusual multi-pointed star flowers. From the author's trailer-breeding programme

'Wonderland', a delightful light-blue violet which has stood the test of time (Granger Gardens, Ohio)

CREATING A 'MICRO-CLIMATE'

The period between potting up the leaf-cutting or plantlet and the time when it is able to stand on its own feet and provide itself with the moisture it needs is critical. If the rate of transpiration can be slowed down and the loss of moisture from the leaf reduced, then the cutting can have more time to establish its own roots. There is one very simple way in which this can be done. We know that warm, dry air will absorb moisture much more readily than humid, moisture-laden air, causing the leaf to dry out quickly and start to wilt. If a humid 'micro-climate' can be created around the cuttings, they will have much longer for root formation which will significantly increase their chances of survival.

This micro-climate may be created around the cuttings very simply; the only equipment needed is a clean polythene bag. Once the cutting or plantlet has been potted and watered in, invert a polythene bag of appropriate size over it and secure the bag to the pot by means of a rubber band. Another method is to place the pot inside a large polythene bag, the top of which should be sealed with string or rubber band above the cutting. The aim is to provide an airtight growing environment with high humidity. If you have been successful in this, you will soon see beads of moisture begin to form on the inside of the polythene. This is quite normal; the cuttings inside will not be harmed by the moisture so long as the sun is not allowed to shine directly on them. The moist air inside the bag will slow down leaf transpiration dramatically, giving the cutting more time to establish a root system that will enable it to be self-supporting. After approximately four weeks the polythene bag may be removed, by which time the plant inside should be able to fend for itself. Once the water-rooted leaf has been successfully transferred to compost, separation and growing-on of plantlets is as described in the following section.

ROOTING IN COMPOST

Leaf-cuttings which are intended to be rooted in compost need trimming back to leave about 1in (25mm) of stalk attached to the leaf. This final trimming should be carried out with a razor blade or very sharp knife, cutting the stalk at an angle as described earlier. They should be inserted vertically into the compost so that the leaf stalk is below the surface and the leaf blade sitting on the top. It will be found that if the cuttings are inserted in pairs, back to back, this will prevent them from falling over or bending over as they grow. With the leaves supported upright in this way, the young shoots will be able to grow away freely when they appear. If you are growing only a single leaf, then support it with a plant label to keep it upright.

No special compost is needed for African violets. Any regular peat-based (ie soil-less) compost will serve the purpose. A low-nutrient compost especially formulated for seedlings and cuttings will be best suited for propagating leaf-cuttings. African violets are shy-rooting plants, unable to penetrate a heavy or compacted compost. It is for this reason that loam and sand formulations (eg John Innes) are not suitable, being too heavy. The peat-based composts, with their light, open texture, are ideal. When filling the plant pot, it is important to firm the compost only lightly,

Leaf-cuttings planted back-to-back in compost

otherwise the purpose of having an open-textured compost will be defeated.

Most African violets are quite happy to spend their entire life in a 3½in (9cm) plastic pot. This same size of pot is suitable for propagating leaves. Fill it to the brim with compost, then lightly firm it. Insert the cuttings as described earlier. The compost should then be watered with tepid water either from above or by standing the pot in a bowl of water for a few minutes. If you choose to water the compost from the top, take care not to disturb the leaves which you have carefully propped up against each other or against a label. After watering, cover the leaf-cuttings with a polythene bag as described on p90. Place the pot in a warm light position, but out of direct sunlight.

The use of hormone rooting powder is not necessary with African violets; in fact, many people have found that this can have a detrimental effect. Once the basic techniques of leaf propagation have been mastered, you may wish to try something different and more adventurous. It has been found that leaf-cuttings taken with only the tiniest piece of stalk attached to the leaf, or even no stalk at all, will tend to produce 'sports'. So, if you fancy a gamble, you may care to have a go; who knows, you may raise an exciting new African violet!

MOTHER LEAF AND PLANTLETS

Once the leaf-cuttings are set into their pots, then comes the time to exercise the virtue of patience. The leaves will form roots in about six weeks; if after this period of time the leaf looks green and healthy, it is safe to assume that it has rooted. This is the time to remove the polythene bag. Without this covering the compost will dry out more quickly, so give water from time to time as required. In a further six to eight weeks new shoots will begin to appear through the compost around the base of the leaf stalk. The first sight of your new violet shoots is very exciting, but you must resist the urge to rush into the premature separation of the plantlets. Wait patiently until the shoots have grown well clear of the compost and formed plantlets which are at least 1½in (38mm) high. While these tiny plants are developing, they will be helped by a little dilute fertiliser added to the water.

The larger the plantlet when separated from its mother leaf, the greater its chances of survival. Many people make the mistake of removing the plantlets when they are too small to survive and then experience bitter disappointment when they die. Be patient and wait until they are a good size; not only will they then have a much better chance of survival, but they will be very much easier to handle. One can fairly say that it is almost never too late to separate young plants from the mother leaf. You may ask why they should be split up at all. Could they not simply be left undisturbed in the pot which would reduce the risk of loss and eliminate the shock of splitting up and pricking out?

Certainly, if there was only one leaf-cutting in a pot, which had produced only one plantlet, this course of action could be followed and the plantlet left undisturbed. Most leaf-cuttings, however, produce several progeny. If these are left to grow up together in the same pot, there will be perhaps

Plantlets growing from leaf-cuttings, 12-16 weeks after planting

four or five plants in one 3½in (9cm) pot. These plants will never have the chance to grow to their full potential of beauty. They will be distorted by over-crowding, their leaves will stick out at all angles, and if flowers are produced, they will be lost in the jumble of leaves.

In growing African violets, especially when they have been raised at home, the aim is to produce a beautiful plant able to realise its full potential. This means that you must give it the space it needs to produce an attractive rosette of leaves, above which it can display its colourful head of blossoms. You can only achieve this result if you ensure that you have a single crown plant. It is for this reason that the risky business of separating the plantlets from the parent leaf is embarked upon.

The time-lag from setting the leaf-cutting to splitting up the plantlets may be as long as six to nine months, depending upon the temperature at which they are being grown. When they reach a size which you judge to be large enough, it is time to move on to the next stage of the propagation process.

Wait until the plantlets are well established before separating

SEPARATING THE PLANTLETS

When the time arrives to separate the plantlets, it is a good idea to allow the compost in the pot to become fairly dry before you attempt to knock out the contents. Place a hand over the top of the pot, avoiding the leaves; turn it upside-down and give the rim a sharp knock on the corner of a table or bench, which should free the ball of compost and roots. If you are carrying out this operation at home, take care not to scatter soil all over the floor. If the compost is dry, it will easily fall away from the root mass to reveal roots, shoots and plants. A really vigorous leaf will produce ten, or on some varieties as many as twenty young plants; more commonly, you will find you have three or four. If you look carefully into the mass of roots, you may also see new shoots there which have not yet broken the surface of the compost.

Each young plant must now be carefully teased apart from the main stem and root system. At this stage of the process, the possession of nimble fingers is a definite advantage. Even so, it may well be that in this separation process, despite your care, some of the plantlets will lose their roots. This is not the disaster it might appear to be. Let me reassure you that when

Mother leaves removed from pot, each bearing several plantlets

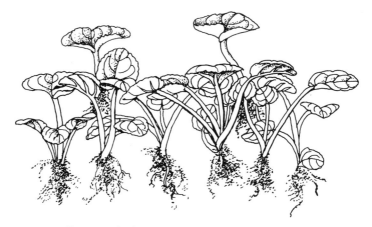

Separated plantlets ready for pricking-out

we use this method of propagation at the African Violet Centre, at this stage we always remove all the roots from the plantlets. This is done to make it easier to insert them into the compost and to ensure that once graded according to size, they can all be expected to grow at the same rate. Thus, when it comes to potting-up time, they should all be uniformly the same size. So you may be assured that the loss of plantlet roots during separation does not matter at all.

When all the plantlets which are big enough for pricking out have been carefully removed, you will be left with the mother leaf, its root-ball and all those potential plantlets which have not yet seen daylight or are too small. Hopefully, your nimble fingers have left them fairly undamaged. In order to produce another crop of young plants, simply repot this root-ball with leaf attached into fresh compost, water in, and cover with a polythene bag for three or four weeks. When these shoots have grown 1½in (38mm) clear of the surface of the soil, the whole process may be repeated.

PRICKING OUT
Handle these tiny plants with great care because they are very fragile. If you have succeeded in producing quite a number,

grade them according to size into groups of three or four. Use 3½in (9cm) pots filled with a peat-based seed and cutting compost, lightly firmed. Into each pot set three or four plantlets, spaced well apart. Make sure that the tiny new leaves in the crown are just above the surface of the soil. Water in with tepid water from above or below, place a polythene bag over each pot, and stand in a warm, light position but out of direct sunshine. There should be clear signs of growth after six weeks, and as soon as you are sure that the young plants are established, the polythene may be removed. When the leaf development has spread to cover the entire pot and the plants begin to look crowded, they are ready for the final stage of the propagation process.

POTTING UP YOUNG PLANTS

It will normally take about twelve weeks between separating the plantlets from the parent leaf and potting them up. In very warm, light conditions, in tropical or subtropical climates, this period of time will obviously be rather shorter. As soon as the group of plantlets in their shared pot have made some sturdy growth and established a strong root system, they will be ready for potting on into a pot of their own. The task of separating the young plants will be made easier if the compost is fairly dry. Knock the root-ball out of the pot and carefully separate the young plants. At this stage try to retain as much root as possible, so take care. Sometimes the roots do seem to be hopelessly intertwined; in this case, use a sharp knife and slice the root-ball into segments much as you would slice a fruit cake. Once separated, the plants are ready for setting into a pot of their own.

For each plant take a 3½in (9cm) pot and fill it with regular, peat-based potting compost. Now that the young plants have a good root system, they can handle a stronger diet and can use a full-strength potting compost. With your finger, or a dibber, make a hole in the centre of the compost, and in it place the young plant. Make sure that the crown is just above the soil surface and gently firm the compost

Plantlets potted three or four per pot

A pot full of bushy young plants ready for re-potting individually

A young plant well established in its own pot, and growing on strongly

Young plants may be top-watered, using tepid-warm water. Take care to keep water away from the crown and avoid spilling on the leaves

around the young plant. Water in with tepid water from below, or around the plant if watering from above. The polythene bag treatment may be repeated for the first few weeks to help the plant to become established, keeping it well away from the direct rays of the sun. Once the plant is clearly growing strongly, remove the polythene bag. Give it as much light as possible now to encourage flowering, but protect the plant from the fierce rays of the summer sun. You may begin to look for flower buds some three months after potting, and certainly within six months you should be rewarded by the beauty of flowers on your own home-grown African violet.

It will probably have taken all of fifteen to eighteen months of patience and tender loving care to produce this colourful result. The months of anxiety and anticipation will undoubtedly be well rewarded and you will experience a thrilling sense of achievement. The pleasure which you will rightfully take in your own success will be added to by the congratulations and admiration of your friends.

Propagation Postscript

Many species of plant may only be propagated at certain times of the year. However, cuttings may be taken from African violets at any season of the year. Certainly the weather conditions in springtime are ideal, with lengthening days, greater light intensity and warmer temperatures ahead. These factors will all contribute towards the rapid establishment of a cutting, so spring is the most favourable time to begin the propagation process.

It sometimes happens that the parent leaf will rot before its plantlets are big enough to split up. Should this happen, it does not spell disaster. Carefully cut the leaf stalk through just above the surface of the compost, leaving the root system to support and nourish the plantlets.

When seeking to propagate variegated-leaf African violets, the normal process as described earlier is followed, but there is an additional point to note on the initial leaf selection. It is

Plant Division

A question that many people ask is whether they can split up a large African violet. There are two possible answers. If the plant under discussion is a very large, single-crowned violet, the answer is that it may not be split up. To slice in half a single-crown plant will be to destroy it.

If, on the other hand, the plant in question is multi-crowned, then certainly it may be divided. Multi-crowned plants fall into two groups. Group one consists of plants which are really a clump of several plants, each with its own root system, probably home-propagated and never separated at the plantlet stage. They will by now have formed a very untidy bushy plant, and will certainly benefit in the long term from separation.

The separation of multi-crowned plants is not as difficult or risky as division (see below), and is carried out as follows. First, the compost should be allowed to dry out so that the plant may be more easily removed from the pot. A further advantage of drying out is that the leaves of the plant will be less fragile. When the leaf cells are bursting with moisture, the foliage is very brittle and will break easily; but when the leaves are somewhat drier, they are more pliable, even slightly rubbery, and therefore much less likely to be damaged in the separation process. This can be most important, because disentangling the leaves is tricky, calling for nimble fingers and a gentle touch.

Once the plant has been knocked out of its pot, much of the dry compost will fall away from the roots. Concentrate first of all on the foliage. Find each separate crown and gently ease it apart from the clump, teasing its leaves free. Once you have separated the top half of the plant, you can then deal with the roots. It may prove quite impossible to disentangle these, and very often the only solution is to take a really sharp knife and cut a section of root free. Keep as much root as possible attached to each plant and do not remove more soil than is necessary. When the plants have been separated, they should then be potted up in the usual way into clean 3½in (9cm) pots containing fresh potting compost and watered in. Although it is not essential, a polythene bag over each pot will certainly help the plants to become established more quickly.

Now we come to the other task, the division of multi-crowned plants which have produced side-shoots which have been allowed to grow and form additional crowns. When this happens, the plant will appear to have several 'faces', and will lose its tidy, symmetrical form. The separation of these crowns requires major surgery, and a high degree of risk is inevitable.

First, allow the compost to become dry, then knock the plant out of its pot and remove from the roots as much soil as possible. This enables you to see clearly the structure of crowns and roots. Take a very sharp knife and carefully slice through the stem below each crown, trying to retain if possible some root with each section. Having removed any tired old leaves from the plants, pot them up in the usual way. After watering in, cover them with a polythene bag for three or four weeks to reduce stress.

Any buds or flowers on a plant to be separated or divided should be removed since all the plant's energy should be directed towards re-establishing its root system. Once this has been achieved, a fresh crop of flowers will soon be produced. On no account should plant division or separation be carried out in the winter. This is a risky operation and winter conditions of light and temperature are not conducive to convalescence. It will be better to wait until spring or summer.

Use a sharp knife to divide an old plant which has produced two or more crowns

tempting to select the whitest, most attractively marked leaves with the aim of producing a new plant with the most eye-catching variegation. Unfortunately, this does not always work out. If you should take an all-white leaf, not only will it not work, but it will turn brown, shrivel up and die. All-white leaves are unable to feed themselves because a leaf must have some chlorophyll (the green colour) in order to manufacture the food by photosynthesis. Therefore, in order to propagate a variegated plant, take as green a leaf as possible, bearing in mind the other criteria for leaf selection.

The general rules of propagation apply to miniatures and micro-miniatures in exactly the same way as they apply to standard-sized plants. Leaf-cuttings are taken in just the same manner, although with such tiny plants the length of leaf stalk will be proportionately shorter.

REJUVENATING A 'STALKY' PLANT

As a mature African violet plant develops and grows older, its lower, outer leaves will die and need to be removed. They

To rejuvenate an old 'stalky' plant, cut through the main stem with a sharp knife

are, of course, being constantly replaced by fresh new leaves growing out of the crown of the plant. After some time, the loss of these outer leaves will begin to expose the underside of the plant and reveal its bare main stalk. This is a natural aging process and is something that we can treat successfully.

When this process of aging first becomes apparent, it is possible to repot the plant into a larger pot, sinking the stalk lower into the compost. This will certainly improve the appearance of the plant for a time, but can only be a temporary measure. Sooner or later more drastic action has to be undertaken in order to rejuvenate a 'stalky' plant. First, using a very sharp knife, slice through the main stalk of the plant just above the soil surface. Trim the stem back, leaving 1½in (38mm) below the last good leaf stalk. Treat as a

Re-plant the top of the 'stalky' plant in fresh compost. Water in and cover with clear plastic to reduce stress, and encourage the formation of a new root system

'Bright Eyes', a beautiful cultivar in the traditional violet colour

'Tessa', a rich purple single from the 'Frilly' series

104

regular leaf-cutting, planting it up in potting compost immediately, or rooting it in water first before potting on. In either case it is most important to cover the plant with a plastic bag to retain moisture and reduce stress. Make sure that all buds and flowers have been removed, and do not give any supplementary feeding for the first ten weeks.

You will find that by this rejuvenation technique, favourite old violets may be given a fresh lease of life, and that very soon they will be flowering again with renewed vigour.

MICRO-PROPAGATION

Another name for the laboratory technique of micro-propagation is 'tissue-culture'. This name tells us quite simply what is involved in the laboratory process. Pieces of plant tissue are placed in culture with the aim of producing new plants. This may sound simple enough, but it is not a technique which can be used at home. It requires a well-equipped plant laboratory, together with a great deal of know-how and experience to produce satisfactory results.

The propagation of young plants by tissue-culture first captured the interest of commercial producers in the early 1970s, when it was shown that many ornamental foliage plants could be successfully reproduced by this method. As the technique has grown in popularity, so the range of plants produced in this way has widened. The advantages of the system are that thousands, even millions, of plants may be grown from a very small amount of stock material in a very short time. So the commercial grower no longer has to maintain a large number of stock plants; that space can now be given over to the production of plants for sale. The young plants are propagated very quickly by micro-propagation, and furthermore they are disease-free. Plant material which is diseased will rot and decay in culture; only material which is free from disease will grow and multiply. So successful has this technique become, that at the time of writing most of the

'Blue Nymph', with its unique pansy-like flowers

107

several million African violets sold in Europe each year are produced by tissue-culture.

The process begins with a ½in (13mm) square section cut from the leaf of the African violet stock plant. This piece of leaf is then sterilised in dilute bleach for 15 minutes before being washed in sterilised distilled water. Having been thus cleaned of potential contaminants, the leaf section is placed on 'agar' in a sterilised jar, and the lid is screwed down. Agar is a translucent jelly-like substance, manufactured from seaweed. To this basic agar material is added a cocktail of hormones which control the growth pattern of the leaf section. The formulae of these hormone additives are the closely guarded secrets of the micro-propagation laboratories. At this early stage of the process, a shoot-inducing hormone is incorporated into the agar, with the aim of inducing rapid multiplication of the plant material.

The jar is placed in a growing room at a temperature of about 70°F (21°C) under artificial lights. Growing rooms do not admit daylight; all the light available comes from artificial sources and its intensity and duration are tightly controlled. After some six weeks the leaf-cutting will be covered with shoots; it will be divided into three pieces and returned to a fresh jar of agar. Within four weeks each of these pieces is ready to be divided again. This process of multiplication can continue indefinitely until the projected stock level has been attained. At this stage the pieces of plant tissue have no roots at all, although they are full of shoots.

For the next stage of the process, the divided pieces are placed in agar containing a different type of hormone, one that will induce rooting. As the plant material begins to form roots, so the shoots will develop into tiny leaves. Within some ten weeks the whole surface of the agar will be overgrown by a mass of tiny African violet plantlets. This bed of plantlets will be very carefully cut up into individual tiny plants and pricked out into compost. This is known as the 'weaning' process. Within seven to ten weeks these 'babies' will have formed good roots in the compost and have grown into sturdy plants ready for potting in the usual way.

For those growers who, like the present writer, also hybridise African violets, micro-propagation is a tremendous help. Our breeding programmes may have produced a particularly exciting new violet, but we have only one seedling plant. Out there are ten thousand customers who would each like to have one for their very own. By the traditional leaf-sticking method of propagation it might well take four or five years to produce a sufficient quantity of plants to meet the demand. The micro-propagation technique will produce within two years all the plants we could possibly need.

For the commercial producer of African violets, modern laboratory production methods offer significant advantages in terms of plant health, speed of growth and reduced costs. But for the violet enthusiast, nothing can match the thrill of taking a leaf-cutting, and by using one's own skill and expertise, producing a plant to be proud of.

5
African Violets from Seed

The miracle of life encapsulated in a seed as tiny as violet seed is one of nature's many miracles. So minute is the seed that an ordinary sewing thimble will hold almost fifty thousand. It is like dust – sneeze, and you will blow it all away! Yet sow it, and in four weeks a tiny plant will have sprouted from that minute seed-shell. In twelve months it will have grown into a magnificent African violet smothered with blossoms. To accomplish this is a deeply satisfying achievement. If, in addition, the seed used was your very own, produced from your own selected crosses, then this must be the most rewarding experience in African violet growing.

The seed-producing process, by means of hand-pollinating selected crosses, is known as 'hybridising'. It will result in seedlings which are unique, new hybrids. This is the way in which the range of African violet form and colour is extended, and flowers with bigger blooms, deeper frills, and more eye-catching shades of colour are produced. There is no great mystery attached to this, no special facilities are needed. A warm room, adequate light and a quiet determination to see it through, are all that is required. There is great pleasure in being able to say of a plant, 'I grew it myself'; but the ultimate satisfaction is to be able to say, 'I created it'.

Hybridising at Home

To make a start on a hybridising programme, all you need are two violets, of differing colours, in bloom at the same time. First, however, you must understand the basis of sexual reproduction in the *Saintpaulia*. Each individual flower possesses both male and female reproductive organs. In the centre of every flower are the yellow pollen sacs, also called 'anthers'. These are the male parts, and, as their name indicates, contain the pollen which will be used in fertilisation.

Protruding above the pollen sacs is the female part of the flower, known as the 'pistil'. When the flower is ripe for fertilising, the tip of the pistil, known as the 'stigma', becomes sticky. When the pollen is placed on this sticky tip, the flower will be fertilised.

At the base of the pistil is the ovary, and within two or three weeks this will begin to swell as the seeds start to form within it. It will develop into a seed-pod which may look very like a green berry. After some six months the seed-pod will start to dry up, shrink and turn brown. The stalk supporting it will also wither. This is all part of the ripening process, and when the pod has become brown and dry, it may be removed from the plant. After a further four-week drying-off period in a warm, dry place, the pod may be carefully opened to reveal anything from 200 to 1,000 seeds.

SELECTING THE PARENTS

Although all African violets contain both male and female reproductive organs, this does not mean that every plant will perform equally as well in the role of 'father' or 'mother'. Experience will show that the pollen sacs of some plants contain very little pollen and that the pollen which is there is non-viable. In other words, it is not effective at fertilising another plant. Experience will also show that some varieties

111

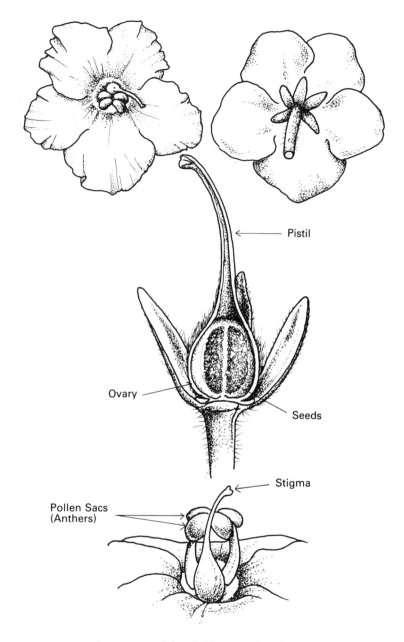

Pistil

Ovary

Seeds

Stigma

Pollen Sacs
(Anthers)

Structure of the African violet flower

will set seed very readily and are therefore ideal for use as seed-parents. There is only one way in which to discover the best varieties suitable for each role, and that is by trial and error.

BREEDING FOR RESULTS

If you decide to do some home-hybridising, you may be content simply to produce seed – any seed – which you can call your own. With a little more planning, however, you can raise your sights somewhat. You could set yourself a target to aim for in your breeding programme. It may be that there are characteristics you like in two separate plants, which you could aim to combine in one flower alone. For example, you may have a blue and white bi-colour, which you feel would be even more stunning if it had frilled petals. You could then cross it with a plant whose flowers are deeply frilled – it may be pink, red or blue. Your aim is to combine the frilled-petal characteristic of one with the bi-colour characteristic of the other. It matters not in the least which plant is seed-parent or pollen-parent, the results will be the same.

From such a cross, there will probably be a wide range of differing flower forms and colour shades. Until the seedlings have been grown into bloom, the results will be unknown. When their flowers appear, you will find that some are frilled and some are plain. Hopefully some will also be bi-colours. If you are really in luck, there may even be a blue and white bi-colour with frilled petals.

RECORD-KEEPING

In order to accumulate information useful in hybridising, it is important to keep a record of the crosses you have carried out. There are two principal reasons for doing this. First, you will learn by results which varieties are best suited for seed-bearing and which make the most effective pollinators. Secondly, if a particular cross produces outstanding results, you will be able to repeat it if you wish to do so.

The normal shorthand way of recording a cross is thus: DELFT × COLORADO, plus the date. The first name, in this case

113

'Delft', is that of the 'mother' plant or seed-bearer. The second name, 'Colorado', is the 'father' or pollinator. If all the flowers on Delft have been pollinated by Colorado, then the cross information can be written on a plant label and inserted into the Delft pot.

BEWARE A POPULATION EXPLOSION

This may be the place to issue a word of caution. At the time of pollinating, your seed-parent plant may have fifteen flowers fully open and ripe for fertilising. It may be that ten of these flowers will set seed, so that if all goes well, in six months time you will harvest ten seed-pods. Each pod will contain on average some 300 seeds, making your total harvest from that plant 3,000 seeds. Until you have sown the seed and raised the seedlings into bloom, you will not know the results of your hybridising. Most of us do not have room to grow 3,000 African violets, and in any event would not want to grow so many plants from a single cross, for although each and every one will be a new hybrid, they will share many characteristics in common.

African violet enthusiasts who hybridise at home normally make several crosses on to one seed-parent. If, for example, there are five flower stems on your selected 'mother' plant, then you may decide to use a different pollinator for each flower stem. Having pollinated the flowers on each stalk, record the cross on a small piece of paper or card and fix it to the flower stem with some clear adhesive tape. If your activities are successful you may still obtain a bumper harvest, but at least the seed will consist of five different crosses.

The Pollination Process

The hand pollination of African violets is best carried out not with a brush, but with the fingers. When the pollen on the 'father' plant is ripe, it will begin to spill from the anthers. Remove these ripe anthers from the flower and carefully tap them over a piece of clean paper to release the pollen. You may then dip the tip of a finger on to the pollen on the paper and place it on the stigma of the 'mother' plant. If receptive and ripe for fertilising, the tip of the stigma will be sticky and some pollen grains will adhere to it. When this happens, the flower is fertilised.

Before proceeding to the next cross from a different pollen parent, it is important to wash your hands to remove any traces of pollen from the previous pollination. If this is not done, parentage will be uncertain. This is the reason why a finger is better than a brush. If several pollinators are being used, a new brush would be needed for each one to avoid the carry-over of pollen from a previous cross. Also, for each pollination, use a fresh sheet of paper.

It sometimes happens that the pollen sacs are reluctant to shed their pollen. In this case the sac may be punctured with a pin to release the contents. If the pollen can still not be shaken out, then the sac itself may be applied directly on to the stigma. Make sure that the pin-hole in the sac is large enough for the stigma to pass through so that it may collect pollen from inside the anther. When it is withdrawn, you should be able to see some pollen grains adhering to the sticky end of the stigma. If this method is used, great care must be taken not to bend or otherwise damage the fragile pistil.

EMASCULATION

Some hybridisers like to remove the pollen sacs from the potential 'mother' flower before it is pollinated. This process is known as 'emasculation', and is done to ensure that the flower is not fertilised by its own pollen. If this should happen, the resulting plants will be of inferior quality. Emasculation should be carried out before the pollen is ripe, otherwise the very act of emasculation can result in the stigma being inadvertently fertilised with its own pollen. In any event, once a flower has been successfully pollinated and the ovary is clearly swelling, then its pollen sacs (if remaining) and petals should now be carefully removed. This is done to eliminate the risk of fungal infections spreading to the seed-pod from the decaying flower material.

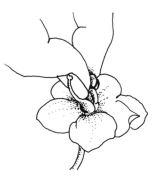

Removing the pollen sacs from the flower – known as 'emasculation'. This is work for nimble fingers or a pair of tweezers

---

THE DEVELOPING SEED-POD

While the seed-pods are developing, maturing and ripening, the plant should be grown on in the normal way. Good light and warmth, and regular watering and feeding, are all important for building up strong pods full of healthy seeds. During this period it is advisable to remove flower buds before they develop so that all the plant's energy is directed to the production of its seed.

The seed-pod will develop quickly, until after six or eight weeks it will look like a green berry. It may be long and pointed, or it may be round – the shape of the pods varies considerably. For some weeks more there will be no change in the outer appearance of the pod, but inside the seeds are growing, developing and maturing. Soon a change will become noticeable. The stalk by which the pod is attached to the plant will begin to shrivel, become thin and may even twist. It no longer holds up the seed-pod proudly, and you may be alarmed by this development. Fear not, it is all part of the normal ripening process. As the stalk withers, so the supply of sap to the seed-pod is cut off, and that, too, will now begin to shrink in size, shrivel and dry up. Soon it will be withered and brown, hanging from the end of the old stalk. When it has reached this stage, it may be removed from the plant. From pollination to harvesting will have taken between four and nine months.

116

Seed pods developing on a flower stalk about four weeks after pollination. Flower petals have been removed as a precaution against disease

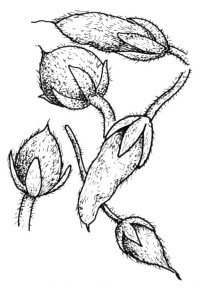

Seed pods vary in size and shape. They may contain from 200 to 1500 seeds each

Once removed from the plant, the seed-pods will benefit from a further drying process. They should be placed in a small cardboard box and put into a warm, dry place. After a further four weeks they will have been completely ripened off and will be ready for shelling.

SHELLING THE SEED

The outer case of the seed-pod, when dry, can be very hard. The easiest way to get at the seed is to cut the pod open using a sharp knife. Before you do this, place a sheet of clean paper on a table and cut open the seed-pod on top of it so that none of the tiny seed is lost. Once the pod is split open, the ripe seeds will drop out on to the sheet of paper. Unless you intend to sow the seed immediately, you will need a small envelope in which to store it. Use a separate envelope for each distinct 'cross', and on it write details, including date of harvest, for future reference. If it is intended to keep the seed for any length of time before sowing, it should be stored in the pod. Seed stored in the pod in this way and then shelled immediately before sowing, has achieved a germination rate of 70 per cent even after four years.

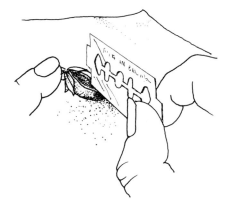

Once harvested and dried out, seed pods may be cut open by a sharp knife or razor blade

Before sowing the seed you will need to have available a suitable container, the appropriate compost, a sheet of white paper, a polythene bag, a plant label and marker pen – and, of course, the African violet seed. Because the seed is so tiny, a small shallow container is best suited for the purpose. You will find that an empty plastic margarine container (½lb/ 250g) will be ideal. Make some holes in the bottom for drainage, then half-fill with a peat-based seed and cutting compost. It is important to only half-fill the container as this

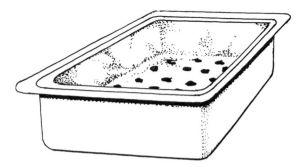

A plastic margarine carton makes an ideal seed propagator for African violets. Puncture the base with drainage holes

Half fill the container with a peat-based seed compost, then soak by standing in dish of tepid water. Drain away excess water before sowing seed

will leave space under the lid or cover for the seedlings to grow. Make sure that the compost is fine, without lumps, and that it is level. In doing this, take care not to firm or consolidate the compost in any way as this will prevent the seedlings from taking root. One cause of the loss of seedlings after germination is heavy and compacted compost. The roots of the tiny seedlings are fragile and can only penetrate the compost if it is loose and open-textured.

Once the compost has been cleared of lumps and levelled, it needs to be moistened. This may be done by standing the container in a bowl containing about 1in (25mm) of tepid water, or warm water may be applied from above using a hand mister. If a mister is used, do make sure that all the compost has been thoroughly moistened, otherwise there will be insufficient water in the compost to carry the seed through to germination. Once the compost has been watered, drained and allowed to settle down, you are ready to sow the seed.

Since African violet seed is so small, it is much easier to sow if you can actually *see* the seed. Before sowing,

Scatter the tiny seeds over the entire surface of the compost. Do not cover with soil or sand. The seeds need light for germination

therefore, assemble the seed on a sheet of plain white paper. This paper should previously have been folded in half, creased, and then opened flat again. If you are using seed from a packet, tip it out carefully on to your sheet of paper. Sometimes the seed is sealed inside a plastic sachet. In this case tap all the seed down to one end of the sachet before cutting open the top with a pair of scissors, then tap out the seed on to the paper.

It really does pay to take this trouble before sowing the seed. You would be surprised at the number of people who complain about lack of germination, but then admit that they could not actually *see* the seed when they sowed it. So how do they know where it fell? Did it fall into the seed-pan, or on to the table? If nothing germinates, there's a pretty good chance that nothing was sown.

This seed is so remarkably tiny, that one may be tempted to think that it cannot possibly germinate and grow into a sturdy African violet. Have faith and press on! Scatter the seed carefully over the surface of the compost in your small seed-tray, trying to distribute it as evenly as possible. This is important so that when the seedlings first emerge they are not overcrowded and have plenty of space to grow during

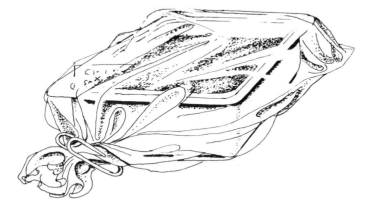

Place the seeded container inside a clear plastic bag, and seal the open end. Stand in a warm room in a light position, but *not* in direct sunlight

their first few weeks without the need for premature pricking out. The creased paper will funnel the seeds into a stream, making it easier to spread them out over the compost.

Once all the seeds have been transferred on to the compost, they must *not* be covered, either with compost or with sand. In order to burst into growth, these tiny seeds need light, so they should not be covered by anything that will exclude the light. So that the seeds and seedlings may be kept moist and humid, the whole container should be placed inside a clear plastic bag and the neck sealed to make it air-tight. Take care to leave a clear space for air between the surface of the compost and the plastic bag, to accommodate the growing seedlings.

The container should now be placed in a warm room in a position where it will receive light, but out of the direct rays of the sun. If the sun is allowed to shine on the seed-tray, it will cook the seedlings inside. Usually a position close to the window on the shady side of the house will be found to be ideal. For germination the recommended temperature is 65°–75°F (17–24°C). Although seed will germinate at a slightly lower temperature, it will take a longer time to do so and results may be patchy. Most good, fresh seed will start to germinate after three to four weeks, but not all the seeds will sprout at once. With patience, you may find that seeds will still be springing to life even three months after sowing, so do not give up on them too early.

Keen gardeners who have a propagator and maybe also a greenhouse, may want to use these to start off their African violets. There is no reason why a propagator should not be used, especially if its temperature control can be set at about 71°F (22°C). Should the propagator be housed in a greenhouse, then great care must be taken to keep sunlight off the seedlings. Unless the greenhouse is heavily shaded, two or three sheets of newspaper should be placed on top of the

---

An un-named seedling with coral-pink blooms

'Celebration', a beautiful sport out of 'Maria', introduced in 1988

122

propagator lid to reduce the light intensity. Even in a shaded greenhouse, better results are obtained when a single sheet of newspaper is placed on top of the propagator.

Raising the Seedlings

The first signs of new life in the seed-tray are tiny pin-pricks of green. When they first emerge, African violet seedlings are very small indeed. Unfortunately, a great number are lost after germination. This frequently occurs as a direct result of the excitement and delight of the growers, who wish to remove the protective cover far too soon. The seedlings have germinated in the warm and humid conditions inside the polythene bag, or under the propagator lid, conditions ideally suited to give them a good start in life. The air inside the container is already laden with moisture, so it does not dry out the tender young leaves, allowing the tiny roots to make steady growth. Remove that protective cover, and the warm moist air is replaced by harsher, more demanding conditions. The air is cooler and drier, which will both slow down growth and place a heavy demand for moisture on the immature roots. It is, therefore, small wonder that when the protective cover is removed too early, many seedlings perish.

In raising seedlings, patience is the key, as it is so often in the activity of violet growing. It is thrilling to see those first tiny seedlings appear from the seed you have sown, but do remember that they have chosen to grow because you provided exactly the conditions they liked. Do not be in a

---

Her Majesty the Queen admires the author's display of African violets at the 1986 Chelsea Flower Show (*Photos Horticultural*)

The author with the actress Susan Hampshire, filming for BBC TV's *Gardeners' World*

The author's African violet display at the 1987 Chelsea Flower Show, for which he was awarded the coveted Gold Medal of the Royal Horticultural Society (*John Wallace*)

Seedlings will usually germinate in four to six weeks, but may take longer

As soon as seedlings are large enough to handle, they may be pricked-out

hurry to change those conditions. The time for acclimatising them to life outside the womb of your propagator or seed-tray will come later. For the present, leave them exactly as they are. Those first seedlings to emerge will thrive and prosper, and as the days go by they will be joined by more and more.

There can be no fixed time when it is right to remove the polythene bag or propagator lid. Conditions vary so much, depending upon temperature, light and the time of year. The process of acclimatisation may be begun some four to six weeks after the last seedling has germinated. The first step is to open the neck of the polythene bag to allow some outside air to get in, but leave the bag itself in position. Then, over a period of two weeks, gradually remove this protection. Keep a close eye on the condition of the seedlings during this time, and if they show signs of shock, replace the cover and return them to the former conditions under which they were thriving.

It may be necessary to water the seed-tray during germination, and this is no problem. So long as the compost was thoroughly moistened before seed-sowing, then, having been sealed in a plastic bag or propagator, it will dry out only very slowly. Should you decide that it does need more water, remove the margarine carton from the plastic bag and stand it in a bowl of tepid water, deep enough to come half-way up the side of the seed-tray. Alternatively, the seedlings may be watered using a hand mister. Fill the mister with *warm* water and apply as a fine spray. Make sure that sufficient water is applied by this method so that it will penetrate down to the roots. Once watered, the tray or carton should be replaced inside the plastic bag and resealed.

Pricking Out

Once the protective cover has been successfully removed from the seed-tray and the seedlings have become acclimatised to 'normal' conditions, you may think about pricking them out. This is done in order that each plant may have sufficient space to grow and develop into a sturdy individual. It is, however, a mistake to give tiny plants too much space. Experience shows that they prefer to be at least within hailing distance of one another. As a rough guide, if a seedling measures ¼in (6mm) across, leave a gap of ½in (13mm) between it and its neighbours. It is true that plants like company, preferably of their own species, but they do need enough space to grow freely.

HANDLE WITH CARE
When African violet seedlings first appear, they are very tiny. If they find the conditions to their liking they will grow quite quickly. Because violet seed is so minute, it often happens

127

that several seeds are sown together, with the result that the germinating seedlings grow together. This overcrowding will lead to distorted leaf development and hopelessly tangled root systems. For this reason it will benefit the seedlings if they are moved apart as soon as they can be safely handled. If you have particularly nimble fingers, you may move these tiny plants as soon as they are large enough for you to hold them. At this stage they are very fragile, so great care must be taken not to knock or crush them.

PROCEED STEP BY STEP

Before lifting the seedlings from their propagation tray, prepare a second tray or margarine carton with the appropriate compost, ready moistened. Remember that it should be only half-filled so that it may be covered and still leave space between the top of the seedlings and the cover. When first pricked out the seedlings should be spaced at intervals determined by their size, as described earlier. A pocket knife may be used to make a narrow planting hole to receive the roots of the young plant. Using the same knife or a plant label, prise each seedling out, taking care not to damage it in

Seedlings should first be pricked-out four or five to a pot. Some weeks later, when they have filled this pot with their leaves, they may be moved on to a pot of their own

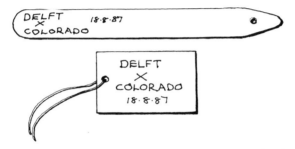

To record your crosses when hybridising, use labels thus. If the entire plant has been crossed with the same pollinator, then a stick-in label may be used. Where each flower stem has a different pollinator, a paper label may be looped over the stem with a strand of cotton

---

any way. With thumb and forefinger, pick up the plantlet by its tiny leaf and lower into the prepared hole, gently firming the compost around its roots. When all the seedlings have been transplanted in this way, water them in with warm water applied as a fine mist through a hand mister. At this stage they will benefit from the return of their protective cover, so replace the lid of the propagator, or cover the seed-tray or carton with plastic film, and return it to its original position.

Once the seedlings have become established in their new home, the protective cover may once again be gradually removed. As they grow, their leaves will spread out until they are touching those of their neighbours. If you leave them for a few weeks longer, the leaves will start to rise up, giving the young plant a 'V' shape. They will be much easier to pot up if left until this stage, rather than potted when the leaves are smaller and horizontal. Once you have decided that the time is ripe for potting up your seedlings, prepare the appropriate number of 3 or 3½in (8 or 9cm) pots, lightly filled with a peat-based potting compost.

Remove each plant from the tray, leaving as much soil as possible attached to the roots. Make a hole in the compost in the pot, lower the young plant into it and gently firm the soil around the roots. Do not use much pressure here, or the

129

compost will be compacted and the young roots will find it difficult to make fresh growth into it. Remember that African violets need an open-textured compost so that their shy and tender roots can make easy progress. Once potted, the plants should be watered in with tepid water (top or bottom), and then placed in a warm, light position out of direct sunshine. If they show signs of stress, cover with a plastic bag for two weeks or so to help the plants re-establish themselves.

A MIXED BAG

From the time of sowing the seed, it will normally take about twelve months to maturity. That is one year's wait for the thrill of seeing the first flower bud open up. There is no doubt that the most exciting seed to grow is that which will produce a mixture of colours. Mixed seed is the result of the type of pollination described earlier, when two differing African violet cultivars are cross-pollinated. The seed which results is known as 'open-pollinated' and will usually produce offspring with a wide range of flower colour and form. Technically, each plant will be a new and unique hybrid or cultivar, in much the same way that every human being is unique and distinct. If you are keen to grow something new and different, then mixed seed is what you need.

The thrill of seeing your first seedling come into bloom is something which has to be experienced. As the plant comes into bud, the anticipation mounts. What colour will it be? Will it be single or double, frilled or plain, self-coloured or a bi-colour? Will it be a new shade never before seen; will it even be the elusive yellow? All will be revealed when that first bud opens up and you gaze upon its beautiful bloom. Whatever colour it turns out to be, I guarantee that you will love it because it is your very own!

6
Displaying Violets in the Home

The way in which African violet plants are arranged in the home can greatly enhance their beauty. It will also increase our appreciation of them. A bunch of flowers, carefully arranged in an elegant vase, will look far more attractive than the same bunch of flowers simply stuck into a jam jar. Similarly, a group of African violets tastefully arranged according to their colours, perhaps with one or two complementary foliage plants, will make an eye-catching feature in a lounge or living-room. No matter in what way we decide to display the plants, it is important that they are at all times clean and tidy, and looking their best.

Grooming Your Violets

If violets are to be kept at their best, it is necessary that they receive regular grooming. This is also the way in which a rapport is built up with plants and your potential to be 'green-fingered' is developed. There are dead flowers to be taken off and old flower stalks to be removed. Dead or damaged leaves also need to be removed and, above all, dust to be kept under control. If the dead and dying material is left on the plant, fungal infections may develop and spread to affect the rest of the living plant. As for dust, this will clog up the working surface of the leaf, inhibiting photosynthesis and slowing down the growth of the plant. Dust on the leaves is also an eyesore; leaves should glow with the rich green sheen of good health.

By attending to the needs of the plants by grooming them, you will become familiar with their sturdy and robust character when in good health, and will soon detect when something goes wrong. Detailed and regular observation will develop your sixth sense.

THE DUST PROBLEM

No matter how house-proud you are, or however clean and tidy you keep your home, dust is everywhere. In fact, the more frequently the vacuum cleaner is put around, or the floor swept, the greater the amount of dust that is disturbed and put into the air. It drifts down and settles on the furniture, the window sills, and of course on to the houseplants. Because African violets have hairy leaves, once the dust has arrived, it stays there and accumulates. Violets growing in the bathroom face the additional hazard of talcum powder, which will eventually turn the leaf from a glowing green to a steely grey. The two ways of removing this layer of dust without damaging the plant, are by brushing or washing it off.

The hairs on the leaf of the African violet grow away from the crown of the plant. If you brush it with gentle strokes away from the centre of the plant, the dust will be removed. It is important to use a brush which is firm enough to move the dust, yet not so hard that it will damage the leaf. A toothbrush or pastry-brush will probably have bristles which are too hard and will score the leaf, damaging the surface tissues. Some writers recommend a camel-hair artist's brush, but these seem generally to be too soft to move the dust. Best results have been obtained with a 1in (25mm) decorator's paint-brush. The method is to support each leaf in turn by placing the fingers beneath it, and, with the brush in the

132

Dusty leaves may be cleaned with a dry paintbrush. Support the leaf whilst brushing gently but firmly away from the heart of the plant

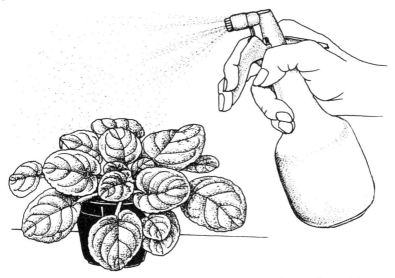

A hand-mister may be used to spray insecticide or fungicide, or plain water for cleaning or humidity purposes. In all cases it is important that the water used to fill the mister is very warm

other hand, make firm but gentle strokes away from the crown of the plant.

This treatment needs to be carried out regularly, and can be quite effective in keeping African violets fresh and healthy. If, however, there is a build-up of dust over a long period, or you have so many plants that brushing each leaf individually is out of the question, then there is another method.

At a recent Chelsea Flower Show in London, the writer's gold medal-winning display of African violets ran into a severe dust problem. The show is staged in a huge 3 acre (1 hectare) marquee on grass and is open to the public for four days. During that time more than fifty thousand visitors a day walk around admiring the spectacular displays of flowers and plants. Fifty thousand pairs of feet soon flatten the grass, and before long the constant pounding of feet begins to raise the dust. At times the air is so heavy with dust that the far side of the marquee is all but obscured from view by this dust-fog. As the dust settles, so the flowers and plants become increasingly grimy. Eventually, in the particular year of which I speak, the dust layer on the African violets became increasingly thicker. So thick did it become that by the close of the show on the second day it was becoming difficult to distinguish between the colours of the flowers. Reds, blues and purples all looked the same dingy brown shade. Pride in the gold medal achievement was rapidly being replaced by apologetic excuses for the drab appearance of the sad plants.

It was quite clear that something had to be done or the proudly displayed gold medal card would appear to visitors on the final day of the show to be singularly undeserved. But what could be done? The exhibit consisted of some six hundred African violet plants, displayed on an island stand measuring 16×16ft (5×5m). Brushing the leaves was obviously out of the question. In any event, that would do nothing to restore to view the lost colours and beauty of the flowers. There was only one option remaining – the plants had to be washed.

Now in order to wash African violet plants, one needs a hand mister. This was the first problem, since we did not have one at the show. However, outside the flower marquee are trade exhibitors, showing off and selling all manner of gardening aids. A manufacturer of hand misters was soon located, a little barter arranged, and in exchange for a couple of violets surplus to our show needs a pump-action hand mister was procured.

The next problem was the water to go into the mister. Tap-water was readily available, but would be too cold and would mark the leaves. At this point a fellow exhibitor came to our aid with an electric kettle. Although installed primarily for coffee-making purposes, this was soon providing hot water for violet washing. A hand mister is ideal for washing African violets because the nozzle may be adjusted to provide a spray of droplets small enough to avoid bruising the leaf or flower, yet with sufficient volume to forcefully wash the dust off the plant.

The temperature of the water used is most important. It must be warm; indeed, if the mister is filled with *hot* water, the resulting spray will be only warm once it is broken up into tiny droplets. At this particular Chelsea show, the African violets were given a thorough washing down on the evening of the second day. The warm water ran off the leaves and flowers, carrying with it the accumulated grime and revealing the true dust-free colours in all their beauty. While carrying out this operation the writer was frequently rebuked by late show visitors, and told that in no circumstances should the leaves of violets be wetted! It is certainly true, as a general rule, that water should be kept off violet leaves. There are, however, exceptions, and this was one of those. So long as warm water is used, and the plants allowed to dry off steadily without being exposed to any sunshine, no harm will befall them. By the morning of the following day the plants were completely dry and ready to smile a colourful greeting at a new show day's fresh visitors. As for those in attendance on the stand, they were once again able to take up their positions with pride, square shouldered and bright-eyed before the card proclaiming 'Gold Medal'.

PLANT COSMETICS

There are a number of preparations available designed to enhance the appearance of houseplants. They are available in liquid and aerosol form, and their purpose is to clean the leaves of plants and impart to them an extra shine. They are the cosmetics of the plant world. These preparations do an excellent job on the rubber plant (*Ficus elastica*), the Swiss cheese plant (*Monstera deliciosa*), and the like, because they have a leaf which is naturally glossy. However, these preparations should not be used on the African violet because its leaves are hairy. For violets there is no finer treatment than that provided by a suitable brush, or a thorough mist-washing with warm water.

BUDS, SIDE-SHOOTS AND A TIDY PLANT

The majority of African violets look their best when grown as a single-crown plant, that is to say, they have one main centre from which the leaves radiate. This gives the plants a neat and tidy appearance with a rosette of green leaves surrounding a head of flowers. The exception to this scheme of things is the 'trailing violet'. By its nature it is multi-crowned, sending out a profusion of strong side-stems which eventually climb over and down the outside of the pot. These side-shoots on the trailers should not be interfered with, otherwise the climbing/weeping character of the plants will be lost.

In order to keep regular violets tidy and single-crowned, it is necessary to remove side-shoots as they appear. Both side-shoots and flower buds grow out of the axil of the leaf-stalk. At first you may find it difficult to distinguish between them. Wait until it is quite clear whether the growth will be a bud or a leaf-shoot. If a side-shoot is allowed to grow and develop, it will form another crown with its own rosette of leaves. Eventually, from the axils of these leaves will come flower buds. This may sound like a bonus, but it can make for a lop-sided plant which many people find unattractive. It

136

will appear to have several 'faces'.

A side-shoot may be removed quite safely, but you must wait until it is large enough to grasp firmly. Then, a sharp sideways tug will remove the side-shoot whole, leaving in your fingers what appears to be a rootless young plant. You may then set this side-shoot in compost, and with luck it will form roots, thus gaining for you another African violet plant.

Arranging African Violets

SAUCERS

The most common way of accommodating individual violets is simply to stand the pot on a saucer or small dish. In this way the surface of the table or windowsill is protected from the damp compost or from the seepage of water out of the pot. This method offers maximum flexibility, allowing the plants to be placed almost anywhere around the home. They may be displayed singly, especially if you have a really handsome specimen of which you are proud. A single, large African violet in full bloom can look most attractive standing in the centre of a small table.

Less striking plants will have their beauty enhanced if they are placed close together to form a group. It certainly helps to have violets of different colours, but it does not matter if the plants themselves are less than perfect. There are times when even the most experienced grower has some plants which are short of leaves on one side, giving it a lop-sided appearance. By carefully arranging five or six violets together, they may be 'dovetailed' into one another rather in the manner of a jigsaw puzzle, so that their imperfections are concealed. You might well be surprised if you knew how frequently a group of oddly shaped plants, carefully grouped together, had collected gold medal awards. A sickly plant in poor health can never be concealed; but a mis-shapen plant in good health can make a real contribution to the beauty of a plant arrangement.

It is very tempting, when violets are in saucers, to water them where they stand. There are a number of reasons why this particular temptation should be resisted. The first of these is a practical one. Water from a saucer can very easily spill over and damage furniture and paintwork. Some folk claim that their violets grow best on top of the television set, enjoying the heat given off when their set is switched on. They may well thrive there, but they should on no account be watered there. Spilled water trickling down into the back of a television set will quickly cause a short circuit, with the risk of explosion and fire. If you must stand something on top of your television set, then make it a family photograph rather than an African violet!

A further reason for not watering violets where they stand on a saucer is that it is a very inefficient way of moistening the compost. Briefly, the compost will either be too wet or too dry, leading to the premature demise of the plant. When the compost in a pot dries out it shrinks – this applies in particular to the peat-based compost which violets like. As it loses water, it loses volume and contracts, shrinking away from the side of the pot and leaving a gap. If the plant is then watered from above, the water will tend to run straight down through the gap and out of the bottom of the pot. The saucer will hold a certain volume of wter, but eventually it will brim over, spilling on to the furniture and causing damage. Not only will there be this trouble, but the purpose of the action in the first place will not be achieved. As the water runs through and down the inside of the pot, it will scarcely wet the compost or roots at all, and the plant will gain no benefit, remaining substantially dry. If some of the roots remain dry for too long, they will die and the plant will be disabled. When the incidence of root death is extensive, then the plant itself will die.

In order to avoid the problem of water running straight through the pot, many people pour water into the saucer. This will certainly moisten the compost at the base of the pot, but will need constant topping up until the entire root-ball is moist, right up to the surface of the compost. Even by the exercise of diligence and patience it is not easy to achieve this from a shallow saucer. When too small an amount of water is supplied, only the very lowest level of compost is moistened. If the rest of the compost remains dry for a long period, root death will occur and the plant will be seriously disabled. A plant affected in this way will appear to be in poor health with small wilting leaves. Its flowers will be carried on stalks so short that they hardly peep out above the leaves. It may linger for many months in this condition. Like a motor-car whose engine is firing on only one cylinder, it will limp along refusing to die, but giving satisfaction to no one. An African violet in this condition will only be saved by a radically improved cultural regime, inducing the growth of a new and vigorous root system.

At the opposite end of the watering spectrum from those who keep their plants too dry, are the plant-lovers whose generosity with water knows no bounds. These are the folk who *always* keep water in the saucer; they are the archetypal violet killers. They are the violet drowners who keep the compost waterlogged in the mistaken belief that such generosity will reap the rewards of plant health and beauty. Unfortunately, their faith in limitless amounts of water is misplaced because compost which is permanently water-logged will cause the death of violet roots through drowning.

The most effective way of watering an African violet when dry is to carry it to the kitchen sink and stand it in a bowl of tepid water. Not only does this ensure that the compost is thoroughly wetted, but it also eliminates the risk of furniture damage and exploding television sets.

TRAYS AND BOWLS
There are available narrow, shallow plastic or fibreglass trays, long enough to accommodate several pots of African violets. They are simply an extension of the saucer method. They enable one to arrange on a windowsill a selection of different coloured violets with the minimum amount of effort. Watering is as recommended for the saucer-based plants.

Flower lovers find it attractive from time to time to

139

arrange African violet plants in a bowl. Plants arranged in this way are better left in their own pots rather than knocked out and replanted together. The reason for this recommendation is quite straightforward. Suppose you have a bowl large enough to contain five African violets; it is unlikely that each of these plants will be equally vigorous in growth. Moreover, some may have a greater number of leaves than others. Therefore, their water requirements will differ. It may well happen that when two of those plants are in need of water, the other three are moist enough. If you water the bowl in order to satisfy the needs of the two dry plants, there is a serious risk of overwatering the remaining three plants which do not need water.

It has been found by experience that plants which are left in their own pots and simply removed from the bowl for watering and then returned, stand a better chance of a long life. A well-cared-for arrangement of different coloured violets in an attractive bowl will make a beautiful and admired centre-piece for a dining table.

POT-COVERS

One of the advantages of arranging violets in a bowl is that by this method the plant pots themselves are hidden. The appearance of single plants can be much enhanced by the use of a decorative pot-cover. This does exactly as its name implies, it covers up the plant pot. Most florists and garden shops carry a selection of pot-covers, from inexpensive plastic ones, through the range of pottery models, to exquisite porcelain containers. Shops selling antiques or bric-a-brac can be a fruitful hunting ground for beautiful old containers.

Saintpaulia shumensis, one of the delightful wild violets from Tanzania

'Ding Dong Trail', a most unusual bell-flowered violet, which aroused great interest when introduced at Chelsea in 1986. (Nicknamed the 'Ding Dong plant'!)

When selecting a suitable container for your plant, it is obviously important to choose one which the pot will fit. The diameter should allow a space between the plant pot and the container wide enough for a finger to be inserted to remove the plant for watering. Also the height of the plant pot inside the pot-cover should be level with the rim of the container. If the pot-cover is too tall, its rim will press on the leaf-stalks of the plant, forcing it into an unnatural attitude. Furthermore, the stalks may be bruised, causing serious damage to the leaf. The rim of the pot-cover should be smooth and not rough, rounded and not sharp.

As for the design or colour of the container, this will be a matter of personal choice and preference. The general rule is that it should not compete for attention with the plant it is displaying, and should therefore be of a neutral or subdued colour. A bright and gaudy pot may be a feature in itself, but put a beautiful violet in it and it will distract the eye of the beholder. The pot is there not to draw attention to itself, but to enhance the beauty of the plant it contains.

It is appropriate here to add another word of caution about watering. If a plant is watered in situ in its pot-cover, it is impossible to see when the water has been taken up. In order to avoid the danger of the plant standing permanently in water, it is safer to remove it from the pot-cover for watering, returning it after it has been thoroughly drained. Before putting a newly acquired pot-cover into use, it pays to check that the base is waterproof. Some pots are made of porous material which will allow water to seep through and cause damage to furniture. It pays to check that a pot is thoroughly glazed at least on the inside. Should you discover that a prized pot is porous, then it can be placed on a saucer or waterproof mat to prevent damage to the standing surface.

TROLLEYS

One difficulty experienced by many violet enthusiasts is a shortage of windowsills in their homes. Houses without

An un-named trailer seedling

windowsills present problems of light for African violets. If there is no windowsill on which to stand them, where can they be placed so that they receive adequate light? One solution to this problem is the dining trolley. Usually mounted on four wheels, frequently double-decked, this can become a very attractive mobile home for a collection of violets. Its mobility is a great asset because it makes it very versatile.

The greatest advantage of using a trolley is that it can be moved into the best possible position for light. In the summer it can be moved to the shady side of the house, to stand close to the window in order to receive maximum light without any direct sunlight. During the winter, your trolley of violets may be moved across to the sunny side of the room to enjoy the winter sunlight. On the other hand, if your home has only sunny windows, a trolley will enable you to keep your violets near enough to the glass for good light, but far enough back from the window to avoid the scorching rays of the summer sun.

The use of a trolley can bring superb results. When the plants on it are looking at their best, you can move your mobile flower-bed to the most eye-catching spot to show them off to visitors to your home. A trolley-load of African violets in full bloom makes a most colourful display, doubly delightful when the garden outside is in the harsh grip of winter.

INDOOR LIGHT GARDENS

African violets make a most striking feature when displayed in an indoor light garden (see p38). Such a unit, placed in a dark corner of a living-room or hallway, can transform the gloom by the brilliance of its light and colour. The bright and colourful flowers, illuminated by their artificial light source, will shine out against the background of their dark surroundings. It is this contrast between the brightly illuminated flowers in an otherwise dark and gloomy corner, which makes it such a conspicuous feature. So long as the light garden is placed in a warm position, the more gloomy and

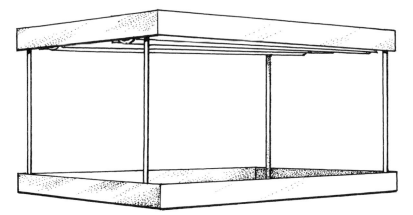

A simple indoor light unit housing two 2ft (60cm) fluorescent tubes. This unit will hold eight African violets in 3½in (9cm) pots, and they should receive 14–16 hours illumination daily

dim the position, the more striking will be the results.

As a means of displaying African violets, the indoor light garden excels; as a light source for growing and blooming violets it may prove less effective than natural daylight. This will be due in part to the composition of the light spectrum, and also to the lower light intensity. In any event, you may find that your plants in the light unit are rather slow to initiate new buds once blooming has finished. One solution to this problem is to circulate the plants. When they have finished flowering, they may be moved out of the unit and on to a windowsill in ideal natural light conditions. Once they have come into bud again, they may be returned to the light unit where they will happily come into bloom. The present writer has found that this system works well and means that the light garden can always be in bloom, a constant source of delight and pleasure.

TERRARIUMS FOR MINIS

Glass terrariums in various designs are becoming increasingly popular among houseplant enthusiasts. The traditional design follows the lines of a miniature greenhouse or lantern, totally enclosed but accessible through a hinged door. By this

Trailing violets in hanging baskets give an added dimension to plant displays in the home, that of height. The best position for these plants to be grown is close to the window on the shady side of the house. Hanging pots or baskets enable this to be done with great effectiveness. Suspended from the curtain track, or hung from wall-brackets above the window, they will flourish. Beware of hanging them at the side of the window, as although they may be close to the glass, they will be shaded from direct daylight by the wall and may not thrive.

A young trailer may be allowed to remain in its original pot and simply placed in an appropriately sized hanging pot. Alternatively, it may be planted up into a suitable hanging container. The growth habit of trailing violets is branching and ultimately pendulous – the stems of the plant grow out and down over the side of the pot, eventually concealing it entirely. This can make the watering of the plant a difficult operation. The growth of stems and foliage will become entangled with the basket and supporting strings, making it virtually impossible to remove the plant. Therefore, the only way of watering it is from above. Inevitably, some water will spill out, so great care should be taken.

Various types of hanging basket are available. The simplest is a plastic container, with three supports terminating in a hook. The trailing violet can be placed in this, still in its own pot, and the hook looped over a piece of cord tied to the curtain track. The most popular and aesthetically pleasing hanging baskets are constructed in macramé work, and allow a variety of containers to be used. Alternatively, small and ornate wicker baskets may be pressed into service, supported by a cord or cords tied to the handle.

Trailing African violets give great scope for imaginative ideas on their display. Just as they may be suspended in hanging baskets, so they may be supported from below as on a pillar. A tall, slender vase into the neck of which a plant pot can be set, will show off a trailer beautifully while holding its pendulous stems clear of the surface.

means it is possible to squeeze a hand inside to cultivate the plants growing there. The most suitable and commonly grown plants in terrariums are miniature ivies, pilea, ferns, chlorophytum, and other dwarf-growing foliage plants.

Large glass carboys are also proving to be popular homes for houseplants. These huge jars have a small neck at the top through which it is possible, though difficult, to attend to the plants. Because of the degree of difficulty in cultivating plants in carboys and terrariums, they are best planted up with foliage plants which are slow growing and require little attention.

At some point it seems that many owners of terrariums and carboys become a little bored with the predominance of green in their glazed gardens and want to add colour by way of a flowering plant. There is no doubt that the very tiniest African violets, the micro-minis like Pip Squeek, look very pretty, decorative and colourful in a terrarium. Before a violet or any other flowering plant is set into a terrarium, however, two things have to be borne in mind. One is the level of light available, the other is the ease with which dead flowers may be removed.

In order to initiate bud development, a violet needs a fairly high level of light intensity. During the wintertime, in temperate zones, this means that it needs some direct sunlight. Unfortunately, a carboy or terrarium exposed to direct sunlight will become warm, the air inside will heat up and there will be a serious risk of cooking the plants it contains. It is therefore most important that such a container is not exposed to the direct rays of the sun, but is allowed maximum daylight on the shady side of the house. Unless the violets in a terrarium receive a sufficient light intensity, they will be unable to flower. This would, of course, defeat the whole purpose of planting them in there in the first place.

The second difficulty about growing violets or any other flowering plants in a terrarium, is that of removing spent blooms. The environment inside one of these glazed mini-gardens is highly suitable for houseplants; cold draughts are eliminated, the temperature is very steady, the air is humid.

147

However, they are also the ideal conditions for the development of fungal diseases such as botrytis. A clinical approach to hygiene is vital if disease is to be kept at bay. All unhealthy growth should be removed, as should any dead or damaged leaves. Probably the major source of botrytis among plants growing anywhere is dead and dying flowers.

In an enclosed container, with extra high humidity, violet flowers will develop botrytis very quickly. It usually starts on the pollen sacs, quickly spreading to the petals. An infected flower head or petal, falling on to a leaf, will soon infect that, too. The spread of the disease is very rapid and can reduce the contents of a terrarium or carboy to a mouldy brown heap within days.

By all means add colour to a terrarium with some mini violets, but do be vigilant. They should be examined daily and any dubious leaf or flower material removed before it can spoil the beauty of your miniature indoor garden.

There is another way in which the tiny mini violets may be shown off to advantage. They look very attractive when planted into a brandy glass or wide-bowled wine-glass. The glass will protect them from draughts and provide them with extra humidity, while the extra height provided by the stem of the glass will show them off to great advantage. Since there will be no drainage, watering must be carried out carefully using tepid-warm water, and only given when the plant is clearly in need.

Violets as 'Pets'

Some years ago a survey was carried out in Britain to discover the attitude of members of the general public to houseplants. The results of the survey astonished the researchers, for it was revealed by their findings that people regard houseplants as pets, along with their dog, cat or budgerigar. It did not require the commissioning of a survey to learn that we talk to our pet animals, we groom and feed them, we take pleasure in their company, are anxious when they are sick and distressed when they die. What was new was that it had not been fully appreciated before that all of these things applied also to the pot plants in our homes.

We have in the past been a little shy about admitting that we talk to our plants. There was a fear that our friends (human) might regard this behaviour as rather odd or peculiar. Yet is there any one of us who can honestly deny that he has never said to a gorgeous violet in full bloom, 'My word, you are beautiful!' Eavesdrop on any violet enthusiast doing the rounds of his or her plants, and you will hear them say, 'Oh dear, you are dry, you do need a drink,' or even asking the plant a question, 'You do look droopy, what's the matter with you today?'. That we talk to our plants is a sign of how much we care about them. They are our friends, they depend on us totally for their life and health, and our love for them is expressed in our attention to their needs.

Just as cats and dogs need grooming, so do African violets. Their leaves need brushing to keep them clean; old flowers and dead leaves have to be removed or the plant will become sick. Animals and plants both rely on us to provide them with water to drink, and both need regular feeding if they are to grow and develop their full potential. We take pleasure in the company of our pets, and the bright and colourful flowers of our pet African violets will lift our spirits and brighten our hearts on a dark and dull day. Their flowers console us when we are unhappy and give us promise of brighter days ahead. Like all pets, their company is therapeutic.

When our pets fall sick, it is natural for us to be concerned and anxious about them. The same holds true for our pot plants. But whereas a dog or cat can be taken to the veterinary surgeon for advice and hopefully a cure, there is no obvious person to whom we can turn when our plants are sick. We are thrown back on to our own resources, or driven to ask the opinion of friends, which means making a public admission of failure. This book itself may make a contribution towards diagnosis and cure, but there is bound to be much anxiety involved.

Even greater distress is felt when a violet of which we have been particularly fond, finally dies. Plants, like animals, have a limited lifespan. They will not live for ever, and we have to learn to accept death as a natural conclusion to life. How reluctant we are to acknowledge this. One has seen many homes in which terminally ill African violets are not allowed to die. What was once a large and vigorous plant, covered with blossoms, has now been reduced to nothing more than a two-leaved stump in the centre of a pot of sodden compost. It has absolutely no chance of survival, yet its owner cannot bear to let it go.

It appears that guilt has a part to play in all this. We blame ourselves that we have failed to keep the plant in good health. In some way we are responsible for its sad condition, we fed it too much or too little, watered it too often or too infrequently, exposed it to frost or the blazing heat of the midday sun. In any event, it is our fault, and we cannot bear to let it die.

There is an old saying, 'If at first you don't succeed, try, try and try again.' If you have plants that reach the terminal stage of life, do them and yourself a favour and let them pass on. You may find you are too attached to the plant or the memory of its former beauty, to shoot it unceremoniously into the rubbish bin. In that case, so long as it is free of pest and disease, dig a hole in your garden and drop it in. Then be brave enough to try again with a healthy new young plant.

The role of the flower in our homes is to beautify our surroundings. When they cease to fulfil this role and look instead like the patients in a horticultural sick-bay, it is time to bid them goodbye. Don't clutter up your home with no-hopers and has-beens. Move them out. Make room for other beauties anxious to brighten your days and lift your spirits.

7
Your Questions Answered

History and Origins

Where do African violets come from? In the wild, African violets occur only in Tanzania, East Africa. They grow there in the district of the Usambara mountains, at varying altitudes up to 7,000ft (2,200m).

When were they introduced to cultivation? They were discovered in 1892 by a German colonial official, Baron Walter von St Paul, who was an administrator in what was then the East African territory of Tanganyika. In that year specimens were sent to his father in Germany where they were successfully grown.

Who named this new plant? This newly discovered plant was officially named by Hermann Wendland, director of the Royal Botanic Garden at Herrenhausen, near Hanover. In honour of its discoverer it was given the genus name '*Saintpaulia*', and because its flowers resembled those of the true violet, it was given the specie name '*ionantha*', meaning violet-flowered – hence '*Saintpaulia ionantha*'. Wendland also

151

gave it the popular name '*Usambara veilchen*' (violet), by which it is still known in Germany to this day.

Is the African violet one of the true violets? The African violet is not related to the true violet (viola). When in 1893 Wendland gave it its popular name, he was only comparing it to the true violet. It actually belongs to the family of plants called 'Gesneriaceae', and its closest relatives are streptocarpus, gloxinia and achimenes.

When were African violets first offered for sale? Discovered in 1892, classified and named in 1893, African violets were very soon available to the general public. Sutton and Sons, Reading, England, 'Seedsmen by Royal warrant to Her Majesty the Queen' (Victoria) were certainly selling seed of *Saintpaulia* by 1894. A letter to them from 'Mr. W. Higgs, Gardener to J. B. Hankey Esq.' states, 'At the October show (of the Royal Horticultural Society 1894) I exhibited some *Saintpaulia ionantha* from seed I obtained from you, and received a First-class certificate'.

Sutton's flower seeds list for 1895 includes '*Saintpaulia ionantha*' thus:

A remarkable new gesneriaceous plant with deep green fleshy leaves in the form of a rosette, from the centre of which springs a cluster of flowers resembling a violet in shape and colour, the individual flowers being about one inch in diameter. Seedlings commence to bloom within 6 months from date of sowing, and continue to flower during the winter months. The plants require the same treatment as Hybrid Streptocarpus. Greenhouse perennial. Height 4 inches. First-class Certificate R.H.S., 1894 ....per packet 2s.6d.

——— *Boys and Girls, Doubles and Trailers* ———

Are 'boy' and 'girl' violets of different sexes? African violets are normally bi-sexual, having both male and female organs on the same flower. The terms 'boy' and 'girl' refer to differing leaf types and have nothing to do with the sex of the plant.

What distinguishes a 'girl' leaf from a 'boy' leaf? One of the original named varieties of African violet was 'Blue Boy', mutations of which produced the first double flower and the first pink-flowered violet. In 1941 a further mutation appeared from Blue Boy. This time it was not in the flower, but in the leaf. The leaves of the mutant plant were not the plain, standard green; they were rounded, thicker, slightly wavy, with a striking pale patch on the leaf-base. This sport of Blue Boy was given the name 'Blue Girl', and ever since then this type of leaf has been known as 'girl-type'.

Who gives violets their names? The right to name a new African violet hybrid belongs to the breeder or raiser. Some names are registered with the African Violet Society of America, which is the international recording authority. Their register runs to many thousands of names, although most of the varieties listed are probably no longer in cultivation.

Which were the first named African violets? In 1927 ten seedlings were selected for naming at the Los Angeles nursery of Armacost and Royston. These are the real originals of the violet world: 'Admiral', 'Amethyst', 'Blue Boy', 'Commodore', 'Mermaid', 'Number 32', 'Neptune', 'Norseman', 'Sailor Boy' and 'Viking'.

Are there any scented African violets? Unfortunately, today neither species nor hybrid violets have any fragrance. If they had it in their distant past, millions of years ago, they have since lost it. Plant breeders see no possibility of breeding for fragrance, the one serious deficiency of the African violet.

When did the first double violet appear? All the wild varieties of *Saintpaulia* have single flowers, as had all the hybrids in cultivation until 1939. In that year a sport of 'Blue Boy' appeared with 'double' flowers. It carried two sets of petals, instead of the normal single set of five.

Why do some violets drop their flowers? This flower-dropping is a characteristic of the *Saintpaulia* species. It doubtless evolved over millions of years as an aid to the survival of the species. If the flower petals drop once the bloom has been pollinated, the seed-pod has a better chance to develop and ripen. If the petals do not drop but remain attached, as they die they will go mouldy with fungal infections. This disease is likely to spread to the swelling seed-pod and destroy it. That plant will therefore find it difficult to perpetuate itself through seeding.

Once the *Saintpaulia* was taken into cultivation for its ornamental attractions, people wanted the flower petals to remain on the plant for a longer time. Also, falling flowers, dropping on to the leaves and decaying there, caused disease problems and made the foliage unsightly. Once the double-flowered hybrids made their appearance, there was the opportunity to breed into the singles their non-dropping characteristic. Today, most singles have non-dropping flowers, but there are still some that retain the typical *Saintpaulia* characteristic of premature petal-drop.

Is there a yellow African violet? The scarlet, orange and yellow areas of the spectrum are at present missing from the African violet colour range. Although yellow violets have been claimed, they appear to have been creamy white rather than a true yellow. Some flowers appear yellowish on the reverse of the petal when in bud, but invariably disappoint when they open up. The present writer has been offering a prize of £1,000 since 1985 for the first buttercup-yellow African violet, but has received no genuine claim for the money. Those who have put in a claim, underestimate his ability to distinguish between a *Saintpaulia* and a primrose!

How vigorous are the variegated-leaved varieties? The vigour of these attractive plants with their ornamental foliage varies. Because the white areas of the leaf are unable to work to support the plant, it follows that the whiter the leaf, the less vigorous is the plant.

Will plants or plantlets with all-white leaves survive? The short answer is 'No'. A plant with no green chlorophyll in its leaves is unable to photosynthesise or manufacture the food it needs through sunlight. When selecting leaves for propagation from a variegated plant, choose the greenest leaves. Even so, some of the plantlets produced may be all white. They are beeing entirely supported by the photosynthesis of the parent leaf, and when separated will not survive.

What is a 'trailing violet'? A 'trailer' is an African violet hybrid which has a branching and weeping or pendulous habit. This characteristic comes usually from *S. grotei* or *S. pendula*, which produce several stems with a vine-like habit. These species, particularly *S. grotei*, are in the ancestry of most modern-day trailers. They are usually grown in hanging pots so that their stems and blossoms can cascade freely down over the container.

────────── *The Way to Successful Growing* ──────────

As a beginner, I find my friends confuse me with conflicting advice. Why? African violets are remarkably tolerant and adaptable. This is most fortunate since people have widely differing methods of caring for them. Their basic needs are water, light, warmth and food; the total absence of any one of these essentials will lead to failure. Within this framework, however, we all have our own methods of meeting these needs. The method which works for one person will not necessarily work for his neighbour. Some swear by top-watering, others by bottom-watering; some recommend rain-water, others use cold tea; some swear by one brand of fertiliser, while others regard that particular brand as a poison. By trial and error you will discover the technique which works for you; for whatever method brings you success with African violets is the right one for you.

How long will an African violet live? The answer to this question depends very much on the care they receive. A very strong claim to the quickest killing of mature violets could be made by a visitor to the African Violet Centre in 1987. Having bought three violets in full bloom, packed in a small tray, she carried them out of the shaded greenhouse and placed them in her motor-car. It was a summer's day of brilliant sunshine and they were placed near the car window to give them the full benefit of the light. She then visited the tea marquee for a little refreshment before leaving. On returning to her car some twenty minutes later, she was appalled at the sight of the plants. Gone were the beautiful flowers, gone the glossy green leaves; in their place were three pots of mushy brown vegetation, rotting and smelly. Twenty minutes was all the time it took the midday sun to scorch those violets to death.

At the other end of the scale, there are a surprising number of people who have kept violets for ten, even twenty years. The longest-lived violet about which the author has heard was over thirty years old.

What is a single-crown plant? A single-crown plant is one which is grown without side-shoots or suckers, alone in its pot. In order to produce a plant worthy of exhibition, it should have one crown or heart, with a complete rosette of leaves encircling a head of flowers. To achieve this desired result, any side-shoots or suckers must be removed as soon as they appear and are large enough to grasp.

Do African violets flower only once a year? Since violets originate from close to the equator and are day-length neutral, they have no seasonal flowering period. They will bloom at any time of the year, and if you are particularly successful you may persuade a plant to bloom non-stop for over twelve months. It seems that light of adequate intensity is the most critical factor in determining the plant's ability to flower regularly. A normal healthy plant may be expected to have at least two flushes of bloom each year.

Sideshoots will distort the shape of an African violet plant

Finger pressure is normally sufficient to remove the sideshoot, which may then be rooted and grown on as a new plant

Why do my flowers come out paler at home? The intensity of light available to the plant will affect the boldness of colour of the flowers. Winter blooms are often paler than summer blooms of the same violet variety. Indeed, in the case of some bi-colours like Miss Pretty, normally white with a pink border, the pink is often absent on winter-flowered plants. The following flush of flowers, in late spring or early summer, will have the normal pink edging.

With violets grown in the home, it is the poorer light which will cause the blooms of the plant to be pale in colour. This is one reason why it is important to grow violets as close to the window as possible. Remember that on the shady side of the house, the light intensity 3ft (1m) away from the window is only one half that of the intensity right there next to the glass.

Light considerations apart, there is no doubt that the regular application of a suitable fertiliser will enhance the colour of violet flowers.

Do African violets need a rest period? African violets do not have a natural dormancy period and, given sufficient warmth and light, will continue to grow and blossom throughout the twelve months of the year. They do not need resting after flowering. Continue to water and feed as normal, and they will soon come back into bloom.

TEMPERATURE, HUMIDITY AND WATERING

What is the ideal temperature for African violets? Violets thrive best in a temperature band of 65°–75°F (18°–24°C). Continuous high temperatures in excess of 80°F (28°C) will lead to loss of vigour, a readiness to wilt, and shrivelled or aborted flowers. Prolonged low temperatures will slow down the growth of the plant, until below 50°F (10°C)

'Porcelain', a popular commercial blue/white bi-colour

'China Cup', a blue/white bi-colour with a difference – the blue centre (from the author)

growth will cease. Below 45°F (8°C) the plant is in danger and the touch of frost causes death.

Will these plants grow in my garden? Unless you live in the tropics, the answer is 'no'. If the climate where you live is frost free and rarely falls below 50°F (10°C) even on a winter's night, you may be able to grow African violets in your garden. They will need to be planted in a shady place, protected from the direct rays of the sun. Alternatively, in a warm climate they may be put out on to a shady verandah during the summer months. If you do decide to plant violets outside, be aware that tropical rainstorms will wreak havoc with their delicate flowers.

Are violets affected by draughts? Draughts of cold or freezing air in the winter will give a nasty shock to an African violet. Continued cold draughts can lead to the plant's death. Similarly, draughts of hot air, blowing on to a violet from a fan-heater, will cause the leaves to shrivel and wither, and risk the death of the plant.

Will they succeed in an air-conditioned room? Air-conditioning appears to have no harmful effects on African violets. On the contrary, by keeping the air temperature down to more normal levels, and reducing excessive humidity, its effects can be seen to be positively beneficial.

Is central heating bad for African violets? By raising the temperature to levels comfortable for human beings, central heating does African violets a favour, too. In fact, they thrive where central heating keeps a room at a steady, even warmth. This is one reason why violets do well in hospitals,

---

The micro-violet 'Mini Marina' at home in an elegant glass bowl

A trolley-load of violets makes a colourful mobile display

A colourful display of violets in an indoor light garden

161

where room temperatures tend to be of a very even warmth. This form of heating will, of course, reduce the level of humidity of the air, which may in a dry climate call for corrective action.

Does gas central heating affect African violets? Here the writer can only speak from his own experience. In a house with gas-fired central heating, a gas cooker and a gas open fire, no adverse effects were seen among the violets being grown there.

What is humidity? Humidity is the degree of moisture present in the air around us. It is measured on a scale of 0–100 by a hygrometer, the normal range being 30–70. In our homes the humidity will be high in the summer, but low in the winter when our heating systems dry out the air.

Is humidity important for violets? In most situations the natural humidity is quite adequate for African violets. If you live in

Additional humidity may be provided by a tray of moist shingle. The water level should always be well below the base of the pot to prevent constant waterlogging

an arid or desert region, it may be necessary to increase the humidity. Similarly, during winter when the air in our homes is being dried out by heating systems, additional humidity can benefit our plants.

How can I increase the humidity? Increased humidity can be provided for your violets by the following methods:

1 By grouping plants together, the humidity in the air around them will be increased.
2 The plants may be stood over (not in or on) a tray of moistened shingle, sand or pebbles.
3 Dishes of water may be placed among the plants.
4 A hand mister may be used to apply a fine spray of warm water to the leaves.

Does it matter if I give my plants cold water? Cold water will cause a shock to a plant accustomed to a tropical atmosphere. But, you may ask, what about the rain that falls on them in Tanzania? For those who have not visited the tropics, and know only the cold rain of temperate regions, it should be pointed out that tropical rain is *warm*.

Cold water spilled on African violet leaves will cause white marks where it has killed the green chlorophyll. Cold water given by bottom-watering will chill the delicate feeding roots and cause brown leaf-spotting. Whether watering from top or bottom, always use warm water. This will not mark leaves, as long as the plant is not in any sunlight.

Will tap-water injure my violets? Despite the chemicals like chlorine and fluoride which are added to water supplies to improve its quality for customers, African violets will take tap-water in their stride. Nor does it seem to matter whether the water is 'hard' (a high calcium content) or 'soft'.

We have a water-softener installed, is the treated water all right for my plants? Water-softeners replace the calcium in the water with sodium. This is poisonous to plants, accumulates in the

Dry violets may be watered at the kitchen sink. The water should be tepid-warm, and about 2in (5cm) deep. Stand the violets in the water for about half an hour, then drain before returning to a dry saucer or pot-cover

compost and cannot be flushed out. Therefore, water for plants should be taken off the water pipe *before* it passes into the softener. Artificially softened water should never be used for watering violets or any other houseplants.

Some people say water from the top, others say you must water from the bottom. What do you say? For all practical purposes, it makes no difference whether you water from top or bottom. What really matters is that you give no water to your violets until they really need it; that you use warm water; and that you make sure you moisten all the compost in the pot.

What harm will come to a violet which stands in a saucer permanently filled with water? The effects of this treatment will be the waterlogging of the compost in the pot. Capillary action will keep the compost saturated and squeeze out the air. Eventually the roots will be drowned, resulting in the collapse and death of the plant. African violets are not pond or water plants.

Should I water my plants in the morning or in the evening? They may be watered at any time of the day, but morning is preferable. In the words of one old grower, 'Don't send your plants to bed with cold wet feet.' If you water early in the day, the plants have a chance to get to work by photosynthesis to start to use the fresh moisture. By the time darkness falls and growth activity ceases, some water will have drained away, some will have been used by the plant, and the compost will be considerably less wet than it was immediately after watering.

How do I tell when the African violet needs watering? The golden rule here is 'Wait till it wilts.' When the leaves lose their normal crispness and begin to droop a little, make sure that the compost is dry, then give your plant a good drink of tepid-warm water.

Which is the best way to water a newly potted young plant? It is better to water in a young plant from the top, giving just enough water to moisten the compost around its roots. Do not saturate the entire pot until the plant has become established.

What about watering violets while I'm away on holiday? If you are away for up to three weeks, give your plants a really good soak before you go, then stand them in a room on the shady side of the house where they will not be exposed to bright light. Even if you are away for three weeks, you should find the plants in good health when you return.

CLEANING, FLOWERING AND LIGHT
How can I clean off the dust from my violets? African violet leaves

may be cleaned by washing or brushing. To wash them, use a hand mister filled with warm or hot water. Make certain that the washed plant is not exposed to bright light until it is quite dry. Alternatively, dust may be removed from leaves by brushing with a standard domestic paint-brush. Support the leaf and make strokes with the brush away from the centre of the plant.

I've spilled water into the crown of my plant, how can I remove it? If allowed to remain, this water could damage the newly forming buds in the crown. Remove carefully using absorbent tissue paper.

Can I spray my violets? It may be necessary to spray violets to clean them, to increase humidity, to apply foliar feed or to control pest or disease. This may be carried out without damage to the plant so long as the water used is warm, and the plant not exposed to bright light until it is quite dry.

Can I use a leaf-shine spray to gloss-up the leaves of my violet? The answer is 'No'. African violets have hairy leaves, and cosmetic sprays will only block their breathing pores and reduce their efficiency. Remove dust with water or a brush to restore the natural gloss to leaves.

My violets are all leaf and I just cannot get them to flower again. Where am I going wrong? The most important single factor in getting violets to bloom regularly is the available light level. In areas of poor light, for example in the centre of a room, the intensity is too low to enable the plant to initiate flower buds. To bring a violet into bloom, place it next to the glass of a window on the shady side of the house (sunny side in winter). Net curtains and venetian blinds reduce light levels so much that they will prevent violets from flowering.

The centre of my plant is congested with leaves. How can I get it to flower? Girl-type violets frequently become very tight in the crown. The removal of two or three leaves from the centre will enable more light and air to reach the crown, and hopefully stimulate the formation of buds.

If you see flower buds having difficulty trying to grow up through the leaves, ease their way by carefully removing a few of the latter.

At what age will a plant first flower? Under normal home-growing conditions, leaf-propagated and seed-grown plants will bloom in about twelve months. Under nursery conditions, plants propagated from leaf-cuttings will flower within nine months, while some seedlings will bloom before they are six months old.

I heard somewhere that I should remove the first flower buds from a new plant. Is this true, and why? When growing African violets to meet a high quality specification, commercial growers will remove the first set of flower buds that appear. This is done to strengthen the plant, so that the second flush of flower buds will provide a stronger and more colourful display on a larger plant. Unless you are growing at home for exhibition quality, there is no need to remove any flower buds. Let them come into bloom, and enjoy them.

Can I place newly bought plants straight into my resident violet collection? No matter how impeccable a source a new plant may come from, treat it with caution. It is wise to quarantine new plants for at least six weeks before letting them mix with your regular violets. Keep them if possible in a separate room, until you are quite sure they are free of pests and disease. One new plant which is host to aphids or tarsonemid mite will quickly spread its infestation through your collection given half a chance – so be cautious.

I know that plants need water, warmth and food, but why is light important? Light enables the plant to manufacture food for itself by the process known as 'photosynthesis'. Without light, or with insufficient light, the plant is unable to photosynthesise, and will die.

How much light does a violet need? Differing plant species require differing light levels. Some of the shade-loving ferns will survive on extremely low levels of light; many other plants require several hours of direct sunshine daily for optimum health. African violets come somewhere in between, needing bright light but shaded from the direct glare of the summer sun's rays.

How can I tell if my violets are getting too much or too little light? Too much sun will scorch violet leaves, turning them yellow. It will also burn the flowers, turning them brown. Too little light will cause the violet's leaves to grow large and lush on long leaf-stalks; it will also be unable to flower, or will produce only a very few pale blossoms.

Can violets ever be exposed to sunlight? Sunlight in the early morning or late evening will not harm African violets. Winter sunshine in temperate zones will be positively beneficial, encouraging flowers in the coldest months.

Can African violets be grown under artificial light? Normal room lighting is of no benefit to African violets as its intensity is too low. However, violets will grow well under fluorescent tubes if given 14–16 hours light daily at a distance of some 12in (30cm) below the tubes.

COMPOST
Do I need a special compost for African violets? No. Almost any peat-based houseplant compost will prove satisfactory for violets.

Are the John Innes formula composts good for violets? The John Innes composts are *not* suitable for African violets. These plants need an open-textured compost to allow their shy roots freedom to grow and develop. Composts based on loam are too heavy and too easily compacted. The growth of violets planted in them will tend to be stunted and the plants will be small in size.

What is a soil-less compost? Soil-less composts are made without the use of any garden soil or loam. Instead they are constructed from peat, sand, perlite, vermiculite, polystyrene granules, etc.

What about all-peat composts? These composts are manufactured from fibrous peat, to which is added a balanced fertiliser to provide initial nutrient for the plants. Trace elements are also added, together with a wetting agent to ensure the rapid absorption of water. These composts are in widespread commercial use in the production of houseplants.

What is the pH measure of compost? pH is a scale from 0 to 14 used to measure acidity or alkalinity. 0 is very acid, while 14 is very alkaline. The acidity/alkalinity of compost may be measured by a pH meter or with special pH measuring strips. African violets seem to prefer composts just on the acid side, with a pH of 6–6.5.

FERTILISER AND ITS USES
If I use a reputable potting compost, why do I need to add fertiliser? The fertiliser which is added to compost during its manufacture supplies the nutrients on which the plants feed as they grow. Newly potted violets require no extra feeding, but after some ten weeks a strongly growing plant will have exhausted most of the initial food supply in the compost. At this stage additional or supplementary feeding will be beneficial.

How do I know which fertiliser to use? It is better to use almost any fertiliser than none at all. If you have a choice, use one that is designed especially for flowering plants. A very reliable standby is a tomato fertiliser. It will not put tomatoes on your African violets, but it will certainly encourage them to bloom. Obviously, the best fertiliser to use will be the one which is specially recommended for African violets.

How soon should I feed newly potted plants? If your plants have been set in a reputable compost-mix, they will not require any fertiliser for ten to fifteen weeks, depending on the vigour of their growth.

Can fertiliser build up in the compost? Regular feeding over a long period can lead to the build-up of fertiliser salts in the soil. This is particularly the case where the plant is always watered from the bottom. A thorough watering from the top once in a while, with warm water, will wash out these accumulated salts, and be beneficial to the plant.

My plants look sick. Will fertiliser revive them? No. If your plants are sick, fertiliser will not help to revive them because lack of fertiliser does not cause sickness in plants. Without sufficient food they will fail to thrive, their growth will lack vigour and their flowers will be sparse. Fertiliser enables a plant to reach its full potential, to grow strongly with glossy green leaves and a multitude of flowers.

Which method of applying fertiliser is best? The type of formulation chosen is very much a matter of personal preference. You may choose between soluble powder or granules, tablets, sticks, mats or liquids, and even foliar feeding methods. It is true to say that every formulation has its advocates – the choice is yours. Read carefully the manufacturer's recommendations, and on no account give a stronger feed than that in the instructions. Unfortunately, in their enthusiasm to sell their product, some fertiliser manufacturers recommend too generous a ration of feed. Half the recommended rate would probably be about right for violets in most cases.

Pots and Repotting

What is the main difference between growing in plastic pots as opposed to the old-fashioned clay pots? The principal difference is in the rate at which water is used up out of the compost. Plastic pots are non-porous, so the only water loss by evaporation is from the surface of the compost itself. Clay pots are porous and allow water to evaporate from the entire surface area of the pot. The result is that a given volume of moist compost will dry out five times quicker in a clay pot than in a plastic one of similar size. Great care must be taken, therefore, to ensure that violets in plastic pots are not over-watered.

Do I need to 'crock' plastic pots? Plastic pots do not need to have bits of pot or stones in the base to cover the holes. This was done with clay pots to stop soil falling through the large central hole and to improve drainage. Plastic pots normally have about four small drainage holes in the base, and a free-draining compost will allow excess water to seep out of these holes.

Can African violets be grown in containers of glass, glazed pottery and metal? Containers of glass and glazed pottery are suitable, as are receptacles made from a non-corrosive metal. The problem occurs with these containers when there is no drainage facility. In these cases it certainly helps to have a layer of stones or gravel in the base to improve drainage for the roots in the compost. Very great care must be taken in order to avoid waterlogging the roots.

What is the best size of pot to use? African violets have a small and fairly shallow root system. For all practical purposes, a 3½in (9cm) pot will be found to be adequate. The shallower 'half' pot or 'dwarf' pot is preferable to the standard-depth one. Plants which are growing with particular vigour may be repotted into a 4in (10cm) pot, but only large specimen plants will need anything bigger than this. Violets seem to be happiest when they are root-bound, and certainly give a better flower performance when they are thus restricted.

The roots of my violet are growing out of the base of the pot. Should I repot it? If it looks healthy and happy, then leave it where it is. Ensure that it receives a regular supply of a suitable fertiliser. African violets like to be pot-bound.

I feel like being generous and repotting my violet into a really big pot so it has plenty of room. Is this all right? Next time you are visiting the florist's, take a close look at the size of pots the commercially grown houseplants are in. They may look small compared to the size of the plant, but you can be assured that the size is right. Most amateur growers repot into far too large a pot. This is aesthetically unsatisfactory because the balance between pot and plant is lost, just as the plant looks lost in such a large pot. More serious is the effect on growth. The roots of the plant cannot utilise all the compost provided, so that unrooted areas of compost remain waterlogged. Before long the whole pot will be waterlogged and the roots will be drowning. To repot into a large pot is misguided generosity.

I have just bought a new violet from the florist. Should I repot it? Perhaps a story here will best illustrate the answer to this question. Some time ago the writer was exhibiting at a flower show in south-east England. Having set up the display, several exhibition-quality plants remained unused, and three of them were presented to the president of the show. They were beautiful plants in full bloom. The following morning he came to thank the writer and to say how much his wife had appreciated the gift; what is more, he had already repotted all three of the plants.

   Those beautiful plants in fact had only been been potted for fourteen weeks and were in their prime; they certainly did not want to be disturbed at that point, and would have been happy in those pots for the next two years. So when you buy a violet from a flower shop, it may well be in need of lots of tender loving care; it is most unlikely to need repotting. Feed it instead.

When is a plant due for repotting? Depending on their speed of growth, African violets will benefit from repotting at intervals of about two years. The compost in the pot will become tired and exhausted and repotting in fresh compost will stimulate the growth of new roots.

How should I repot a plant? The compost of the plant should be just moist, neither too wet nor too dry. Invert the pot, covering the surface of the compost with a hand. A sharp knock of the rim on a bench or table will free the root-ball. Tease off the old compost around the sides, together with any dead roots. Try not to disturb the very heart of the root-ball. Once the excess roots and compost have been removed, place the plant in the centre of its new pot. The new pot may

To remove a plant from its pot, place the fingers of one hand over the top of the compost (below the leaves). Turn it upside down, and with the other hand remove the pot. If it is reluctant to come away from the compost, a sharp knock against the corner of a table will usually free it

well be the same size as the old pot – the main purpose of this exercise is to provide the roots with fresh compost. They don't necessarily need a larger pot. Indeed, if there has been a large amount of root death, it may be better to replant into a *smaller* pot.

Having centred the root-ball in its new pot, make certain that the base of the crown is about ½in (13mm) below the rim. Carefully add compost around the edge of the pot until the desired height is achieved. Make certain that the crown is not buried in the compost, or trouble will result. Press it down gently, not too firmly. If it is too hard and compacted, the roots of the plant will have difficulty penetrating it.

Water the plant in from the top with warm water, giving sufficient to make the compost moist but not too wet.

Seed Production and Sowing

What is a hybrid? A hybrid is the result of a cross between two parents which are demonstrably different from each other.

What is a sport? A sport is a new plant, propagated vegetatively, which differs significantly from its parent plant. This mutation occurs as a result of a sudden change in the properties of a single gene. Leaf-cuttings made without any stalk remaining give an increased chance of mutation. A cultivar which has a tendency to sport will generally do so at an increased rate when subject to micro-propagation by tissue culture.

When selecting plants for cross-pollinating, does it matter which one is selected to be the 'mother'? It makes no difference which plant in a cross is 'father' (ie, provide of pollen) and which is 'mother' (ie, seed-bearer). The results will be the same. However, some plants prove more reliable at setting seed than others and these would naturally be selected for the 'mother' role.

There is an exception to this rule about interchangeability. The exception applies to variegated-leaved African violets. In

174

a cross between a variegated and a non-variegated violet, the progeny will only have variegated foliage if the variegated parent is used as the seed-producer. In other words, a variegated seedling can only come from a variegated mother. But even then there are exceptions, when green-leaved plants will produce variegated offspring by mutation from a leaf-cutting. It is all part of the fascination of these beautiful plants.

Can the average violet-lover expect to produce worthwhile new hybrids? African violets do not discriminate between professional and amateur breeders. Professional growers have the advantage of being able to grow many more seedlings into bloom, thus enhancing their chances of breeding some outstanding new violets. Keen amateurs have had their successes, too. Two African violets which are very popular in Britain at the time of writing are 'Delft' and 'Silver Milestone'. Although both were introduced by the present writer, they were hybridised by an experienced amateur violet collector, Joan Hill, in her own home. The results of her labour of love now adorn and beautify the homes of thousands of violet-lovers.

Do I need a 'boy' and 'girl' plant to hybridise? No. The terms 'boys' and 'girls' refer to a certain leaf type and have nothing to do with sex. All African violets are bi-sexual and may be used to fill the role of 'father' or 'mother'.

What are the male parts of the flower? The anthers or pollen sacs are the male part of the flower. They provide the pollen to fertilise the female organs.

What are the female parts of the flower? The stigma and ovule are the female parts of the flower. The stigma is the tip of the pistil which receives the fertilising grains of pollen. After fertilisation, the seeds begin to develop in the ovule, at the base of the pistil.

175

Do African violets ever revert? Yes, they certainly do. Bi-colours in particular are inclined to lose their edging.

Will there ever be a yellow African violet? So far as we know there has never yet been a really yellow African violet flower. Since the plant is capable of producing yellow, as is evident from the bright yellow of the pollen sacs, it may be that one day a mutation will occur which will result in yellow petals also.

What is a 'star' flower? The 'star' flower appears to have five or more petals. In fact, the African violet flower consists of one petal only, with five or more 'lobes'. Star-types have five identical lobes, each with one pair of pollen sacs. Star flowers tend to be large, and with their five pairs of bright yellow anthers can be most striking.

When can I pollinate? Pollination may be performed at any time of the year, although high summer is best avoided. The most important factor is the ripeness of the pollen. At the African Violet Centre we pollinate from September on-wards, through the English winter. Seed is harvested from mid-April onwards.

What are the simple mechanics of pollination? The process involves transferring pollen from one plant on to the stigma of the 'mother' plant. This can be done very simply by removing ripe pollen sacs from the 'father' plant and, with a pin or sharp razor, splitting them open. Place a finger on to the exposed yellow powder (pollen) and then dab a little, carefully, on to the stigma of the 'mother' plant. If this flower is ripe to receive pollination, the stigma will be sticky and some pollen grains will adhere to it. It has now been pollinated. The rest may be left to nature herself.

I can't believe it is that simple. How do I know if my pollination 'worked'? If the pollination was successful, within two weeks the ovule at the base of the pistil will be clearly seen to be

176

swelling. When this is seen, very carefully remove the pollen sacs and petals from that flower. It will soon develop into a little berry; this is the seed-pod.

How long will it take the seed-pod to mature? This usually takes from three to six months.

When should I remove the seed-pod? When the pod is ripe, it turns brown, shrivels up and shrinks in size. The stem supporting it will also wither. When this happens, remove the pod and dry it indoors for a further four weeks.

How do I remove the seed from the pod? The ripe pod should now be dry and hard. Slit it open with a sharp knife and you will find inside several hundred tiny seeds.

How many seeds will be in one pod? The number varies a great deal, depending on the size of the pod. Some cultivars produce a small seed-pod containing, maybe, two hundred seeds. Other violets produce a large pod containing well over one thousand seeds.

How soon can I sow the seed? This may be sown immediately after shelling. Fresh seed gives the highest germination percentage. The longer it is stored, the poorer germination will be achieved. African violet seed appears to keep best if left in the pod and shelled shortly before sowing.

What is the best container to use? Top favourite for seed-sowing is a ½lb (250g) plastic margarine container. Make some drainage holes in the base. Up to two hundred seeds may be sown in each container.

I have a lovely warm airing cupboard. Can I place the seed container there to germinate? Definitely not. African violet seed needs light to germinate. While it would certainly appreciate the warmth of your airing cupboard, it will not germinate in the dark.

How soon will violet seed germinate? Really fresh seed in ideal conditions will germinate in fourteen days. More usually, it takes four weeks, but seeds will still be bursting into life after three months.

When can I prick out the seedlings? They may be pricked out just as soon as they are large enough to handle.

What colour can I expect from my own seed? This will depend on the colour make-up of the parent plants you used in your cross. The odds are that each separate cross will produce not just one colour, but a range. It may be blue/white or it may be pink/red, or some other combination. It is the unpredictability of this which makes hybridising violets such a fascinating activity.

New Plants from Leaves

Is it true that you can grow an African violet plant from a leaf? Yes. This is the normal way of multiplying violets and is known as vegetative propagation. The plants raised in this way will normally exhibit all the characteristics of the parent plant.

Does it matter which leaf I use? Some people say a round leaf will not work, and that I should use a pointed one. The shape of the leaf makes not the slightest difference. In any case, their shape varies according to variety, and all stand an equal chance of rooting. What does matter is that it is a healthy and vigorous leaf in good condition, free of damage or disease.

Which is the best way to root a violet leaf? Some say root it in water, others say root it in compost. The choice is yours. Success is achieved with either method.

Why has my healthy leaf not produced any baby plants after six months? If your leaf has rooted, and after six months looks healthy but with no sign of plantlets, the chances are that the leaf selected was too old. It may still produce results and should be kept for at least twelve months. Best and quickest results are obtained if a younger leaf is used.

Why do some leaves I try to root rot off? Make certain that the final cut on the leaf-stalk is made with a razor-blade or really sharp knife. If the stalk is crushed or damaged in any way, then it will become infected with a fungus disease and die off.

Do I need to use a rooting powder? No. When propagating African violets by leaf-cuttings, no rooting agent is normally used. They root quite freely, without any artificial aid.

What is the best time of year for taking cuttings? This will depend to some extent on your own local climate. In temperate zones, springtime is best for cuttings, because the warm, light days of summer are ahead, which will aid the growth of the plants.

How soon will my leaf form roots? If you root in water, you may watch and time this for yourself. First roots will appear within two or three weeks, and a fairly extensive root system will be established within six weeks. When rooting leaves in compost, they are usually well established within six weeks.

How soon will tiny plantlets appear? Baby plants will begin to peep out of the compost after ten or twelve weeks, although in highly favourable conditions they may appear even earlier.

How soon can I transplant the plantlets? They need to be big enough to fend for themselves before you separate them. Many people lose plantlets by transplanting them prematurely. Wait until they are at least 2in (5cm) high before you attempt to remove them from the mother leaf.

How long does it take from a leaf-cutting to achieve a plant in bloom? The answer is, quite a long time. Leaf propagation is slow, but if you have patience you will find it very rewarding. If you produce a plant in bloom within twelve months, then you've done very well. With some people it takes as long as two years.

What colour will the flowers be? Leaf-cuttings produce plants with the same characteristics as the parent plant. If your leaf came from a blue-flowered plant, it too will have blue flowers. Occasionally, a mutation will occur, resulting in a sport which will differ in leaf or flower from its parent.

Problems

Why do African violets always die on me? African violets don't just 'die' on people; if they die prematurely, it is usually as a result of something their owner did to them. Most violets which meet an early death are usually drowned by their owner. It is very easy to stop the violet killing – just make sure you do not give any water until the plant wilts with drought.

Why are my violets all droopy? They're probably drowning. Check the pot: if it is heavy and the compost is moist, then the plant needs drying out; if the pot is light and the compost is dry, then your plant is asking for a drink.

My violet has grown right up in the middle with a tall stalk. What has gone wrong? This is a normal part of the aging process. New growth comes out of the crown of the plant, the old outer leaves die off and are removed, and eventually the plant has a 'trunk'. Initially, you can conceal this by repotting and sinking the plant lower into the compost. However, it will continue to rise up, and the only solution then is to slice across the stem and reroot the entire plant.

I can never get African violets to flower again. What should I do? The most important factor in bringing violets into bloom is *light*. The chances are that your violets are never given sufficient light to enable them to bloom. Move them to the window on the shady side of the house where they will get full light without the glare of the sun. Net curtains and venetian blinds reduce light levels so much that they will prevent violets from flowering.

My violets have whitefly. How can I get rid of it? In the writer's experience, whitefly do not attack African violets. The white specks on violet leaves usually misidentified as 'whitefly' are, in fact, the cast skins of tiny aphids feeding on the plant. Treatment with a systemic insecticide will kill the aphids, and the white specks may be washed or brushed off the leaves.

Parts of my violet are rotting with a grey mould. What is it and what can I do about it? Botrytis is a fungal infection which will colonise any damaged plant material and rapidly break it down into a mushy slime. Remove all infected material and treat the plant with a fungicide designed to kill the botrytis fungus.

My plants have developed brown spots on the leaf. Is this a disease? Brown marks on violet leaves are frequently caused by watering with cold water which damages the delicate feeder-roots. Once the leaves are damaged in this way, botrytis will frequently come in as a secondary infection. Ensure that you always water with warm water, and that you do not keep the base of the pot standing in water.

Patches of white powder have appeared on my violet leaves, flowers and stems. What is it and what can I do about it? Your plant is a victim of powdery mildew, a very common fungal infection. Treat with a fungicide, diluted with warm water and apply through a hand mister.

What causes the centre of my plants to become tight and bunched up, with tiny brittle leaves? It sounds very much as though your plants are playing host to the worst pest of African violets, tarsonemid mite (also known as cyclamen mite). This tiny creature, invisible to the naked eye, feeds on the newly

181

forming shoots and buds in the very heart of the plant. It is resistant to all regular treatments available for use in the home. The infected plants should be wrapped in plastic and disposed of.

Why are the leaves of my violets turning a yellowy-brown colour? They are clearly being exposed to light which is too bright for them. The sun bleaches the leaves, causing them to lose their normal green colour. Move the plants to a window on the shady side of the house, where the light will be more to their liking.

The flowers on my violet have developed brown specks and streaks and some have shrivelled up entirely. Where have I gone wrong? This is the effect of sunlight on the flowers – it is too bright for them. Move the plants to a window away from the sun.

Why do the leaves of my violets grow so large, with long stalks and no flowers? Your plants are struggling to grow with insufficient light. Move them to a lighter position, but not into the direct rays of the summer sun.

The leaves of my violet have developed white spots, streaks and blotches. Is it a disease? These white marks are where the green chlorophyll has been killed by cold water or exposure to cold air or draughts. It is not a disease, it will not spread, and it will not occur again if you eliminate the cause.

Can you explain the difference between contact and systemic insecticides? Contact insecticides only kill the insect if they come into contact with its body. Systemic insecticides circulate in the sap of the host plant, poisoning the pest as it feeds. Contact insecticides kill by direct action; systemic insecticides kill by indirect action. Insect pests feeding deep in the heart of a plant, or tucked away under the leaves, may escape the spray of a contact insecticide; however, they will certainly not escape the systemic insecticide, wherever they are feeding.

List of
Popular Named Varieties

The master list of the African Violet Society of America records many thousands of named varieties. Most of these are no longer in commercial cultivation, having been superseded by improved cultivars with larger flowers, increased vigour, better petal-markings, and so on. Any list of named African violets has a limited value therefore, and should be treated as a guide only, as it rapidly becomes out of date. To add to the confusion, it often happens that violets exhibiting the same flower characteristics and leaf form will be known under different names in different countries. An example of this is the magenta–edged frilled-white called in Britain 'Fancy Pants', and in the USA 'Nevada', whilst in New Zealand it is known as 'Kiwi Dazzler'.

The following is a guide to some of the popular cultivars available within the various groups at the date of publication.

Standard Violets

PINK SHADES

Maria	Clear bright pink single, frilled petals. Mid-green foliage.
Rococo Pink	Iridescent pink double, with girl-type leaf.
Swan Lake	Large, deep-pink blooms. Petal edges are ruffled.
Marguerite	Huge pale-pink star flowers, wavy petals.
Georgia	Deep-pink single with dark-green leaf.

WHITE

Garden News	Full double white, ruffled petals. Centre occasionally suffused with palest lilac. Light-green foliage.
Sleeping Beauty	Single white, ruffled petals.

183

White Disco
Floriferous pure-white double blossom with sturdy, glossy, medium-green foliage.

BLUE SHADES
Bright Eyes
Rich dark-blue single with prominent yellow anthers, with dark-green leaves.
Wonderland
Large light-blue semi-double blooms, with olive-green wavy foliage.
Delft
Huge semi-double cornflower-blue blossoms over mid-green foliage. Strong grower.

PURPLE-MAUVE SHADES
Tessa
Rich purple single with frilled petals. Prolific blooms carried high over lush mid-green foliage.
Fusspot
Full double blooms of lilac, with deeper colour on the frilled edges.
Summer Spice
Double lilac star flowers with purple specks and streaks.

RED (SHADES OF MAGENTA)
Colorado
Magenta frilled single, lush mid-green foliage.
Kristi Marie
Semi-double dusky brick-red star with occasional white edge. Dark standard foliage. Strong grower, but shy bloomer.
Kingwood Red
Large semi-double blooms of red held over light-green foliage.

————— *Bi-Coloured Standard Violets* —————

RED AND WHITE
Fancy Pants
Top favourite at the African Violet Centre. Superb frilled red-and-white single. Striking flowers held above standard foliage.
Silver Milestone Star
Huge star flowers of magenta, pencil-edged with white. Single.
Mystic Moment
Eye-catching white-edged semi-double magenta flowers. Deep-green foliage. Vigorous growth habit.

BLUE AND WHITE
Ballet Silver
Deep royal-blue single star. Large flower with bold white edge. Mid-green quilted foliage.

Porcelain	Single white flower with vivid blue markings, over light-green foliage.
China Cup	A profusion of single white star flowers with blue centre and blue edge to petals.
Blue Nymph	Unique pansy-like flowers, blue and white two-tone.
Alabama	Single white, frilled petals edged in blue.

PINK AND WHITE

Harlequin	Frilled white blooms edged and splashed with magenta-pink. Deep-green foliage.
Celebration	Large single white flower, its ruffled petals banded with rich pink. Eye-catching.
Miss Pretty	Frilled pale-pink-and-white single with pale-green foliage.

——————————— *Trailing Violets* ———————————

Starry Trail	Masses of large creamy-white multi-pointed star flowers. Contrasting dark foliage.
Magic Trail	Semi-double pale-pink star flowers cascade down over quilted, mid-green foliage.
Ding Dong Trail	The first bell-flowered trailer. Pale-pink single bell-flower with deeper tone in throat. Mid-green, pointed foliage.
Midnight Trail	Multi-petalled mid-blue star. A profusion of flowers over light-green foliage.
Dancin' Trail	Deep magenta-red double stars cover dark-green, red-backed trailing foliage.
Shimmering Trail	Large, lavender double stars in abundance cover medium-green foliage.

——————————— *Miniatures and Micros* ———————————

Pip Squeek	The original micro-violet, smallest in the world. Tiny plant with free blooming pale-pink flowers. Diameter of plant 2½in (6cm).
Sprite	Single white micro, often with a touch of blue. Crisp, sparkling light-green foliage.
Mini Marina	Rich mid-blue single flowers on micro-miniature serrated girl-type foliage.
Pixie Blue	An abundance of violet-shaped flowers in blue. Miniature, diameter 5in (12cm).

185

────────────────── *Variegated Leaf Violets* ──────────────────

Tommie Lou   Double white blooms, light orchid in the
                    centre. Dark-green foliage streaked with
                    white. Introduced in 1967, easy to grow and
                    vigorous in habit.

Midnight   Royal-blue semi-double flowers with white
   Romance   edge. Variegated foliage.

Summer Silk   Shell-pink double flowers contrast with
                    pencil-edged variegated foliage.

Saucy Sunset   Bright fuchsia-red single star flowers above
                    green-and-white variegated foliage.

Royal Lady   Velvety-purple semi-double star flowers with
                    white edge. Leaves have elegant pink edging.

Fancy Trail   Semi-double pink-flowered trailer with shiny
                    variegated leaves.

Suppliers and Useful Addresses

United Kingdom

The Royal Horticultural Society
Vincent Square
LONDON SW1P 2PE
Tel: 01-834 4333

The Saintpaulia and Houseplant Society
Mrs F. Dunningham MBE (Hon Secretary)
33, Church Road, Newbury Park
ILFORD, Essex IG2 7ET

Tony Clements' AFRICAN VIOLET CENTRE
Station Road
Terrington St Clement
KING'S LYNN, Norfolk PE34 4PL
Tel: 0553-828374

The African Violet Centre is open daily throughout the year from 1 February to 23 December, including weekends and public holidays. Visitors are welcome, admission is free, and a wide range of African violet plants and sundries are on sale. Some 500 coach parties are entertained each year. Groups may arrange to visit the showhouse for a talk and demonstration. Party booking details, visitors' leaflet and mail order list available on request.

United States

African Violet Society of America
P.O. Box 1326
KNOXVILLE
Tennessee 37901

Fischer Greenhouses
Oak Avenue
LINWOOD
New Jersey 08221
Tel: 609-927-3399

Granger Gardens
1060 Wilbur Road
MEDINA
Ohio 44256
Tel: 216-239-2349

Lyndon Lyon Greenhouses
14 Mutchler Street
DOLGEVILLE
New York 13329
Tel: 315-429-8291

Tinari Greenhouses
2325 Valley Road
Box 190
HUNTINGDON VALLEY
Pennsylvania 19006
Tel: 215-947-0144

Bibliography

Robey, Melvin J., *African Violets, Queens of the Indoor Gardening Kingdom* (A. S. Barnes 1980)

Wilson, Helen van Pelt (ed), *African Violet and Gesneriad Questions* (Van Nostrand 1966)

Tinari, Anne, *Our African Violet Heritage* (1975)

Fogg, H. G. Witham, *Begonias, Gloxinias and African Violets* (John Gifford 1967)

Sunset Books. *How to grow African Violets* (Lane 1951)

James, Theodore Jr, *How to Select and Grow African Violets* (H.P. Books 1983)

Index

190

Rejuvenation, 103–4, 107
Repotting, 104, 172–4, 180
Reverting, 176
'Rhapsodie', 14
'Rococo', 15; 'Pink', *51*, 183
Roots/rooting, 54, 58, 68, 71, 72,
84–92, *85*, 95–7, 101, 102, 138–9,
163, 171–4; powder, 92, 179
Ruggeri, Peter, 15

'Sailor Boy', 13, 153
Scale insects, 58, 66–7, *72*
Sciarid fly, 72–4
Scorching, 24, 35, 39, 42, 44, 168
Seed 79, 110–25, 174–8; pod, 116–
18, *117, 118*, 154, 177
Seedlings, *123*, 125–30, *126, 143*,
167
Sideshoots, 102, 136–7, 156, *157*
'Silver Milestone', 175; 'Star', *87*,
184
Sowing, 119–25, *119, 120, 121*, 177
Spraying, 166
Spring tails, 72, *74*
'Sprite', *52*, 186
St Paul, Baron von, 9, 10, 151
'Starry Trail', *88*
Stigma, 111, 115, 175, 176
Streaking, 75
'Sunset', 7
Suppliers, 187–8
Suttons, 13, 152

Tanzania, 9, 10, *11*, 17, 28, 39, 151,
163
Temik, 59
Temperature, 20, 26–7, 38–44, 57,

78, 80, 102, 108, 122, 147, 158,
161–2
Terrariums, 145, 147–8
'Tessa', *105*, 184
Thrips, 58, 64–6, 73, *74*
Tinari, Anne/Frank, 17
Tissue culture, 81, 107–9, 174
Trailing, 7–8, 17, 40, 136, *143*, 146,
155, 185
Transplanting, 95–7, 179

USA, 16, 59, 187–8; AVSA, 16,
153, 187

Variegated leaf, 7, *33*, 100, 103,
154–5, 174–5, 186
'Viking', 13, 153
Vine weevil, 71

Wangbichler, Ed, 13
Washing, 63–4, 134–6, 166
Water, 25, 163–4, 181; softener,
163–4; rooting in, 84–9, *85*, 179
Watering, 19, 21–8, 89, 92, *99*, 100,
120, 127, 130, 137–40, 143, 146,
148–50, 155, 163–5, *164*, 170, 174,
181; over, 19, 22, 57, 139, 150,
171
Waterlogging, 19, 22–3, 139, 165,
171
Wendland, Hermann, 9, 10, 151–2
'White Lady', 15
Whitefly, 62, 181
Wilting, 22, 23, 41–2, 139, 165, 180
'Wonderland', *88*, 184

Young plants, 25, 28, 165